# IN DURANCE VILE

# IN DURANCE VILE

by

## John Brown, D.C.M.

*Revised and Edited by*

JOHN BORRIE

**ROBERT HALE LIMITED**
LONDON

ISBN 0 7091 8980 X


Robert Hale Limited
Clerkenwell House
Clerkenwell Green
London EC1R 0HT

Photoset in Great Britain by
Rowland Phototypesetting Limited, Bury St Edmunds, Suffolk
and printed by St Edmundsbury Press
Bury St Edmunds, Suffolk
Bound by Weatherby Woolnough, Northants

# Contents

# Illustrations

## PICTURE CREDITS

# Foreword

Had John Brown been a British officer this story could never have been told. Had he been aggressive he would certainly have spent the duration of the war in Colditz.

He was quiet-spoken, a friendly person, a big man in every sense of the word, with a ready smile, a ready wit, and a way of making friends in most unlikely places, even with Germans in wartime. He was a man to whom one was instinctively drawn and in whom one could establish trust. It was these qualities that allowed him, as a prisoner-of-war in Germany, to follow his own private line of activity to the $n$th degree. He had the unusual facility—by his personality—of making and taking opportunities.

When I was a patient in Lamsdorf Hospital, having been captured in Greece in 1941, I heard of John Brown because he had written an article in the P.O.W. paper *The Camp* explaining the good things that British P.O.W. life in Germany had in store for those who thought deeply. This was a deliberate act with a deep-seated purpose. As such it made him suspect in the eyes of his British P.O.W. colleagues and the German authorities hoped he would join the ranks of the traitors William Joyce and John Amery.

I first met John Brown at Blechhammer E/3 on 21st August 1942 when I was Medical Officer. I wrote, "He had a warm handshake, friendly smile, and a keen intelligent eye. He was 6 feet 2 inches tall, broad and round. He wore battledress and the colourful Royal Artillery dress cap".

I lived with him and the Senior N.C.O.s, and in that barrack room one sensed his steadying influence on camp discipline and camp welfare. His business skills helped many P.O.W. welfare causes.

We had much in common and were immediately drawn to each other. I liked having him as a travel companion on my many weekly trips to outlying P.O.W. camps, to specialist medical clinics, or on shopping expeditions. His constant support at all religious services in the Camp was heart-warming.

When he had the opportunity in 1943 to establish at Genshagen, Berlin, a P.O.W. camp for British who had worked well for Germany, those of us in the know realized this was merely a front to hide his further secret activities there. His charm, his methods and assumed naïvety led him far, even into the German Foreign Office and into the Berlin State Opera House.

Late in 1944 the Nazis realized what Brown was really up to. But they started their witch-hunt too late and by incredible good luck he managed to keep ahead of his pursuers until he reached England.

John Brown was a man of great courage, character, integrity, and with an ability, by his quiet personality, to follow events to their logical conclusion. That he escaped Gestapo revenge is a miracle.

This is an incredible yet true story, now told in full for the first time.

John Borrie, M.B.E., E.D., C.H.M., F.R.C.S., F.R.A.C.S.
Associate Professor Thoracic Surgery
Otago Medical School, New Zealand

May 1980

# I

# *Stalag 8*

"Blimey," exclaimed a P.O.W. next to me as we left the forest and saw the Stalag, "thought I recognized the flaming walk through the trees. It's Lamsdorf! I spent three years here during the first war. Half starved, we were, and kicked if we didn't jump to their bloody orders!"

They hustled us into a large square. The sight confirmed the guards' claim that there were 3,000 Allied P.O.W.s at Lamsdorf alone. Hundreds of men in R.A.F., Navy or Army uniform pressed up to the camp wire, shouting, "How long have you marched, where were you captured, have you had any food, what war news?" until angry guards moved them back.

"Watch out," one of them yelled, "here comes Smokey Joe to welcome you—he's a right sod."

Three German officers entered the compound. "Boys—attention!" shouted the youngest in English, climbing steps on to a platform.

"Now then, you crowd of English bastards, you'll have to learn while in Germany to respect our officers. When they approach, you must stand to attention and salute them. You're all rogues and scoundrels, and unless you behave yourselves, you'll be very badly treated. But if you show that all English are not rotten through and through, and are willing to work hard for our German Reich, you'll be allowed home some time after we've won the war. Your King and Queen have already left England, and within a few days the Cabinet goes too!"

"You bloody liar!" roared a voice from the crowd.

"Stand up the man who said that—I'll have him shot straight away." No one moved. "Unless you stand up at once I will stop rations for the whole camp." At once every single man stood up.

Smokey Joe was dumbfounded. But another officer who we soon learnt was Camp Kommandant called him down and said in German how pleased he was. The English had shown "true discipline" by standing up at the end of his speech. Delighted with unexpected praise from his senior Smokey Joe did not disillusion him.

Later they gave us barley soup and potatoes, bread and cheese; but the unaccustomed food upset our weakened stomachs and there was a dash for the latrine—an open trench near the wire, beside the main road. Here, to ease our agony, we sat on one long wooden pole, bare backsides facing the road which had laughing children lined up on it. To provide their fun this way was the last straw in our degradation.

After we had washed and shaved—by borrowing razors and soap from those still carrying them—they marched us to another compound to record all personal details. I said I was an office manager. They said that was useless in Deutschland. They put me down as a labourer. They next issued postcards to send home, like army active-service cards where one crosses out everything not relevant.

When the long registration of so many was through they told us we would sleep in stables till other barracks were ready. The Germans had been surprised at the size of their "catch"—they had not expected a tenth of the P.O.W.s taken after such a short war. It was June 1940, and the Belgium blitz had started just one month before. Already Lamsdorf held 5,000 P.O.W.s.

I found a corner in the stables where I settled down and started talking to the man next to me. He was C.S.M. Fred Neeve, Royal Corps of Signals, captured near Oudenarde. To my surprise he said he'd been in the army for nearly twenty years. He was different from most regulars, far removed from the bawling sergeant-majors I knew. He saw me looking at his C.S.M. badge and said, "You must realize that the Royal Signallers is a technical unit; rank is gained by seniority of service and skill." We talked ourselves to sleep; here was a kindred spirit.

As I dozed off and the straw warmed up dozens of fleas woke for a midnight feast on me. Next morning when I stripped off my shirt, seeing fat lice, I threw it down. Another P.O.W. grabbed it; fleas did not worry him.

After "breakfast"—a slice of bread and mug of ersatz coffee—Fred Neeve and I walked round the barbed wire where we met many we knew, unaware they had been marching with us. In Neeve I felt I had found a friend who would be close to me whatever would befall us.

In the days that followed we played cards, exercised on the sand, or went for barbed-wire walks; but as the weeks wore on I felt the monotony would drive me mad. The prospect of being in Stalag much longer was intolerable.

When they moved us into new barracks—double-ended huts with wash rooms between—we found beds in three tiers, but only loose straw to sleep on. With memories of the stable lice Fred and I slept on bare boards. The cold showers in the centre worked, and though we rarely had soap we could at least keep clean.

The food was just sufficient to keep us on our feet; we felt dizzy if we moved suddenly. Trouble grew when the Germans decided to give each barrack its daily quota of food to be divided amongst the P.O.W.s by the senior N.C.O. The daily ration was two slices of black bread, four or five small potatoes, about half a pound, a mug of soup—or rather coloured water—plus ersatz coffee or mint tea, twice a day. At every meal one man, thinking his potato smaller than the others, would protest. Then in came the Germans, delighted to see us quarrelling amongst ourselves. They deliberately kept our rations low, then lured us on saying how much better fed were prisoners when they went working for Germany. Some men became so hungry that they asked to go out working, but most resolved to resist authority till forced to do so. It was like passing a "hunger-strike sentence" on themselves. They sat endlessly on devising menus they would eat when they first got home. Food was one topic from morning to night, completely displacing sex as top barrack-room theme. We all felt the same—no desire, no urge, no strength for any sexual exertion, nor was there any opportunity—we were all soft and safe.

I had a pressing reason for starting work. I knew that if I stayed in Lamsdorf much longer my brain would rot: I wanted to keep mentally fit.

During the previous winter, shortly after jumping from bombardier to Q. M. for my battery, which seemed rapid promotion after only ten weeks on active service, I had been

sent to a secret training course with other N.C.O.s. I kept
remembering the officer's words, "If you get taken
prisoner, you can probably be of very great use to us—in fact
far more use than you are now!" I spent hours thinking over
the instructions given to us of what to do once inside
Germany. I kept turning everything over in my mind to
make sure I had the method of communication perfect.

And so, when I heard that a working party was being
formed for Blechhammer, Upper Silesia, where a petroleum
plant would be built, this seemed the very place for me. It
would surely be a mine of useful information.

According to the Geneva Convention a senior N.C.O.
need not work; but the Germans so far had shown no con-
cern to observe the convention. But in fairness this matter
was not helped by many "phoney senior N.C.O.s" suddenly
appearing. The Germans thus demanded definite proof of
rank before they allowed anyone to refuse work. Badges of
rank alone were not enough. As most P.O.W.s had destroyed their Army pay-books when captured, it was difficult
indeed to prove rank. Fred and I both had ours, but he was as
sick as I of wrangling over rations. We thus made no protest
when our barrack was paraded by the guards for civilian
chiefs to pick their slaves.

"*You* need not go if you don't want to," the fat Feldwebel
said. "You're senior N.C.O.s, and we warn you the work
will be hard; but the food will be good."

Subtle propaganda this, for most men forgot about the
hard work part and thought only of good food. But my mind
was already made up. I wanted to go to Blechhammer.

The next morning—Sunday—as we were preparing to
leave Lamsdorf, the whole camp was assembled on check
parade. I thought it must be another church service like
we'd had a week back, when one prisoner preached a sermon
in which he demonstrated that Hitler was a biblical villain
who would in so many days fall while the hosts of good in
the world would triumph. Unfortunately there were
Germans in our midst, dressed as Tommies, and as soon as
the service was over, the man was whipped into solitary
confinement. But this time there was no church service.
The Colonel spoke:

"Gentlemen, I've a very important announcement for you
which should gladden your hearts. It may mean that in a few

weeks the war will be over, and then perhaps some of you will be on your way home, that is, if our beloved Führer decides he does not need you in Germany. Gentleman, *Paris has fallen*, and *France has capitulated!*"

We were stunned by the news; there was a weird ominous silence. Then the murmuring started and it was generally agreed that the Colonel was just another bloody German liar. But deep down, remembering the shambles we had seen in France, many of us felt that it was true.

With heavy hearts, we lined up to march to Lamsdorf station.

Our cup of woe was not yet full for at the camp gates we were handed copies of a newspaper called *The Camp*, published in English for P.O.W.s. The leading article described how the British Expeditionary Force had been completely routed in France and detailed the fiasco of the retreat from Dunkirk. Now that France had capitulated German troops were waiting at the coast for orders to cross the Channel and bring to heel the capitalist criminals in England who had started the war. Once England was occupied the whole world would be at peace, and the beloved Führer would have fulfilled his divine purpose. When the war was over many workers would be needed on the Continent: as P.O.W.s we must expect to remain in Germany: the Germans, as always, would be kind to their captives; we could write home once normal posts were resumed.

The prospect was grim—agonizing. We felt our little world had ended and that we were marching to slavery, for five years—ten years—maybe for ever. In our misery our English spirit revived: spontaneously to a man our column sang "The White Cliffs of Dover".

As cattle trucks took us further east from our world towards Blechhammer, I thought of my home and family and all I had left behind. In the years ahead, would it be possible to be of use to England? I thought back to my training course. "You'll be dealing with a lot of half-wits; you have absolutely nothing to fear," our instructor had said. But he had also told us it was very easy to be made a P.O.W.: all you had to do was walk over the top and forget to come back!

There had been nothing gallant about our shambolic retreat across France: the washing never had been hung out on the Siegfried Line. We had never been that far forward.

# 2

# Long March to the Fatherland

"''ere's 'ow we'll string 'em up," read the caption, "when we meet 'em on t'other side!" strung to underpants stretched on lines across Southampton streets.

Through March 1940 we kicked our heels there, sailings postponed for "technical reasons". But *we* knew better: we'd heard Lord Haw-Haw broadcasting from Berlin each evening asserting that our division—soon to leave England—and our crack anti-tank regiment would never make the other side. But when we finally landed in France on 9th April in the biggest convoy yet, stretching from Calais to the Belgian border, our contempt for the Germans increased to a dangerous complacency. In Outersteine I sat in luxury billets sipping champagne, thinking that all those hours spent on the secret N.C.O. course were totally useless. By December the Germans would be on their economic knees. Nor could they survive when all they had were cardboard tanks and no fuel to get their planes airborne. All our tank-trap digging seemed futile, except that the men needed something to keep them happy by day. But for friendly females by night many would have been driven to despair.

However, by early May there was an expectant glow in the air; rumours were rife. Then the Germans invaded Belgium, claiming that we had violated her neutrality by allowing British officers to cross the border. That night our main body with the guns moved forward, leaving me to collect my B-echelon, no easy task with half of the men tenderly saying farewell to their loves, the other half stoned in the *estaminet*. Adolf Hitler was at last on target.

We reached the Oudenarde Canal near the front line. No one now grumbled at digging slit trenches, though all knew "Hitler couldn't put a plane up!" But we were concerned to learn that the Germans had crossed the Albert Canal, a major obstacle; and by the time we had blown the Oudenarde Canal bridges German troops and transport were across.

Our heavies opened fire; the bedlam lasted thirty-six hours. Then we moved forward to the canal to gloat over the damage. Though our infantry also had had casualties we were confident the Germans were finished.

Next day we were in the mess-room with our franc-in-the-slot organ playing merrily, when a heavy drone—a German plane like a chugging old steam train—flew overhead.

"Just a spotter-plane trying to find our strength," said an officer casually. "We've had orders *not* to fire: we don't want to betray our positions!"

Next morning I was crossing to the mess, unconcerned that the plane was back again. Then came the crash. Aghast I saw a huge crater where the mess-room had been; our organ still moaned on in pain.

Shelling continued all through that day and night; the ground was ploughed up and landmarks swallowed up in clouds of dust. When the firing eased, I saw the Battery Captain who ordered me to remove all ammunition trucks to safety near the Regimental Head Quarters (R.H.Q.). Welcoming a break from a shelling we sped back to park the cars in a forest near Roussell.

Bad news awaited our return. "The Germans are over the canal: our hard-pressed infantry is retreating towards us!"

"We must support them as best we can," said the Major. "If need be we'll fight to the last man. Get those ammo trucks back now and man the anti-tank guns."

So back we went. This time the journey was more perilous, with many hair-raising escapes, but we reached R.H.Q. whole, and I reported to the O.C. He raged and said he'd have me arrested if my news was false. The Germans had *no* artillery and *no* planes: it was absurd to talk of fighting to the bitter end. Just then a loud crash outside brought a white-faced lieutenant in to report that the cookhouse had collapsed on the midday meal. The Colonel lost confidence. He asked me to show him the latest positions. More shells landed while we pored over the map.

The German heavies had found new positions at least four miles on our side of the canal. My own battery was in grave danger. I asked leave to get the ammo trucks back to them; but was ordered to stay put and defend R.H.Q. Armed with rifles we awaited the oncoming German might.

Next day the remnants of four batteries reached R.H.Q. with harrowing tales. On 20th May we retreated further. In an attempt to find a more strategic position my own battery left the rest. But wherever we went, the Germans were there before us. Twenty times the Luftwaffe attacked us in our demoralized retreat across Belgium. "Strategic withdrawal" came over the B.B.C. The Cockneys called it a "bloody fiasco".

Mile after mile refugees jammed the roads—pitiful scenes—but our orders were, "Help no one whatever on the road."

By 25th May we were back in Outersteine, our guns in a semi-circle ten miles ahead and R.H.Q. well behind us.

On 26th May I had to take a food truck up to our gun crew at Merville. When almost there we ran into machine-gun fire that silenced our two guns. We drove on. Merville was chaotic, being bombed and shelled so intensely that we retreated into a cellar with frightened villagers. Most were famished and all were delighted with the rations meant for our gun crew. At dusk we decided to run the gauntlet on that ambushed road, but first found the local undertaker and barricaded our trucks with tombstones. We left one side of the town as the Germans entered from the other side. Locals pleaded to go with us but had to stay.

Nervously we drove without lights, towards the machine-gun trap, and sure enough they opened fire; but the bullets bounced off the tombstones. Seconds later we crashed into a wrecked truck already caught coming in the other direction. There we were, sitting ducks in the middle of the trap. Discretion was the better part of valour: we dived into the ditch.

We crept across fields, tracer bullets flying overhead, Verey lights shining brightly above. Then we found guns which we thought were German. But the men manning them challenged us in English and rigorously questioned us. They thought we were Germans disguised in battle-dress, and were only released after much talking and threats of being shot.

At 2 a.m. we were again in Outersteine. It had been a five-hour hike. The Battery Captain, surprised to see us, told us that five minutes after we had left, he heard the road to Merville was under fire and the town evacuated.

Next morning we moved to Caestre, and the guns placed in the fields, while B-echelon was left in an old farmhouse near a crossroads. After some time I went to report to the Major at his H.Q. near the guns. Rounding a bend and seeing two strange tanks on the road, we quickly dismounted and crept forward. There was no sign of life near the tanks; they were French. Where then was the enemy, especially as the tanks had been silenced by anti-tank shells fired from behind us? At H.Q. we learned these French tanks had been put out of action by our own anti-tank guns, for they were flying their tricolour in the wrong position and our orders were to fire at anything not identified as friendly. We returned to the farmhouse for further orders.

On 29th May I was called by the Major at dawn and told to take my men to the coast. News was uncertain: they doubted if Dunkirk or Calais were still clear: if we asked as we went we could not go wrong: R.H.Q. had already packed bags and gone home: but the Major would stay until the bitter end.

We left before 6 a.m. with goodbyes to the gunners, the Sergeant-Major and two officers—all that we now had left. Because no officer could be spared, I would take charge of the convoy. We drove through the village of Caestre, and even at this early hour one of the locals gave us a few parting shots. The village looked eerie in the half light, several buildings bombed out and wallpaper fluttering on gaunt walls. About a mile further on we found a crossroads, where our instructions were to turn right. As a precaution I sent a dispatch rider (D.R.) ahead, telling him to go at least two miles. When he reported back that the road was clear we started once more. Within 300 yards of all, hell was let loose. The D.R. had been allowed through; we were a much tastier target.

The windscreen shattered over my head. Behind me our own Bren guns and rifles opened up: our only hope was to drive on. But a lorry headed straight for us. With a crash the two trucks locked fast. Figures in blue-grey ran around us. Outside the cab door a nasty German pointed a nastier automatic at my head. I reached for my revolver determined to have at least one shot before he killed me. But my driver grabbed my arm.

"Don't do that, Quarter. For the sake of us all put your

ruddy hands up and surrender! We're hopelessly out-
numbered."

We got out of the truck and had the satisfaction of seeing
some Germans dead. Our Bren guns still spluttered fitfully,
but tanks by now appeared; my fighting days were over.

I looked down the road to see our back lorry reversing and
men from the truck in front running to board it. The
Germans fired as one man jumped on: his head rolled off his
body. The lorry dashed on down the road and round the
corner to warn the gun crew of their danger. I later learnt
that half of those in that truck were dead when they reached
the Major.

In our party those still alive were lined up against the
wall. Six Germans pointed their Schmeisser guns menacingly at us, while others counted their dead and injured.
An N.C.O. reported to a senior German officer, "Sieben-
undsechzig [sixty-seven] dead and wounded." Quickly I
worked out that we had started out with fifty-seven; thirteen
of us were prisoners, and six had perhaps escaped by truck,
so our total losses were about forty—not bad when we were
so disadvantaged.

Then the German officer turned on us. "This morning
you English swine have killed many men who were defend-
ing their country." (He seemed to have forgotten this was
*not* Germany.) "You did *not* fight fairly; later on you will pay
the due penalty." I glanced at our trucks, wrecked and
burning at the roadside and remembered all my good
friends I'd never see again. The Germans shouted and
bawled; for a few minutes it looked as though we would be
summarily dealt with.

Nonchalantly I lit a cigarette, trying to make myself appear at ease. "Why are you smoking?" an officer roared in
German. "Is it because you want to steady your nerve before
we finish you off?" I tried to look confident and ignored his
rage, implying I did not know any German. He rained abuse
on me, waved his arms in the air, abruptly said *"Heil
Hitler"* and went away. He returned with a Sonderführer
who asked in excellent English if I was the senior member
of those captured and what regiment was I from?

"I can't tell you."

He smiled pityingly. "I'm going to take you to someone
who will *make* you talk."

They bundled me into a staff car and I prayed I would have strength enough not to divulge any secrets. The car sped along the road straight in the direction of our own guns, and then turned down a narrow lane to the German head-quarters. I calculated we were within 250 yards of our guns, but years later I learned that they had been abandoned a few minutes after we left, my major and gun crew all safely reaching England.

They marched me to the German Kommandant and with-out warning knocked me down. I was told I'd been insolent, smoking in the presence of a representative of the Führer: I was *not* standing to attention and had thereby insulted the German uniform. The Kommandant asked several ques-tions that I refused to answer. How could I admit to our utter chaos? He then asked, "Where is the rest of your unit, and where will we find the remainder of the B.E.F.?"

"I hope by now they are all on the way home, and out of your reach," I said.

He struck me down again declaring furiously that if I cheeked him again he would have me shot *sofort* (at once).

After more questions but little response he whispered to the officer who had brought me in. They bundled me back into the car.

I felt utterly bereft, like a condemned man walking to the scaffold. As the car sped along, those last moments seemed very sweet to me. I closed my eyes, prayed for God's for-giveness and asked Him to care for my wife, Nan, and little daughter Marion. At least I knew my secret would die with me; and that gave me a little comfort. But I was trembling as I walked slowly from the car helped by a revolver stuck in the small of my back. The rest of the P.O.W.s were still standing, hands raised above their heads. A moment later another young German officer came over and said in perfect English, "You know what is going to happen to you now?"

"Of course I do. Your men have already told us. Because you have lost men fighting against us, you are going to shoot us. We know Germans shoot all prisoners."

"Don't be stupid. Our beloved Führer would never allow us to do that. You are wrong about being shot. You are going on a very long walk—all the way to Germany. You'll be guests of the Führer till we've won the war."

For a time I was not sure whether to be glad our lives had

been spared. I loathed walking, and the prospect of walking several hundred miles in army boots and greatcoat was grim. Also, I had cut my foot in the last few weeks and it still had not healed.

The officer spoke again. "If you've any kit in the truck go and get it, but warn your men—if anyone attempts to escape he will be shot!"

I found my kitbag intact and a bottle of wine I'd picked up in Caestre. They let me keep it. But most had no kit left—all lost in the flames.

My numbed mind began to function again, and I remembered *that course*. "You are absolutely covered by the Geneva Convention," said the instruction. "Hitler will not dare to break its terms. As soon as you are picked up you will be whisked right out of the firing line, and you will soon be in touch with us." Nice words said from a distance; but not one of those clever fellows lecturing us said how to surmount the strain of a very long walk. A bayonet pricking my backside urged me to start walking now!

We moved off east. Germans yelled in front, beside and behind us. Tanks and trucks driven by maniac Germans churned up dust as they coasted perilously near us. If we tried to jump clear, they clouted us with rifle butts.

In an hour we reached a tiny village set in beautiful countryside. They gave us no time to admire scenery: they hustled us straight into the church. It was badly bombed and weird. The crucifix and Virgin were intact, surveying a thousand P.O.W.s in British and French uniforms, sprawled out trying to rest. Some lay on the altar steps, some on the altar itself, others in the pulpit and down the aisles, and some on the pews. The air was blue, hazy with smoke: on all sides P.O.W.s munched their last rations.

The Germans said, "Rest till noon, then you march twenty kilometres." We found a spot in the Lady Chapel where the lamp, still burning on its altar, showed the sacrament was preserved there. We stretched out, not caring that we were desecrating this holy of holies.

At 11.30 a.m. they woke us up shouting, "*Raus*—up! up!" They prodded any who slept with bayonets or rifle butts. The church emptied. Outside they lined us up in fives, English in front, French behind. Whereas many English were sparsely clad and carried no kit, the French without exception, had complete uniform, greatcoat and pack, including blankets—as though they'd left home with time to prepare for a P.O.W. life. We thought the French had let us down by coming out of action too soon: doubtless they thought we had run away leaving them to be caught.

A strong detachment of guards watched us with several motor-cyclists and trucks in attendance. The Germans set the pace and seemed to enjoy themselves. For eight hours we carried on under the relentless sun. Some captured without boots had to walk in bare feet. All were painfully thirsty in the sweltering heat.

At St Pol, French women placed buckets of clean water along the roadside. All the men made frantic attempts to get it, those with water bottles filling them, while others unashamedly knelt and drank their fill. The women rushed to refill the buckets, but a Nazi officer ordered the guards to kick the buckets over. "Let the English swine go without— they can die of thirst and hunger for all I care!" The women protested: the guards brandished rifles and bayonets. A few women resisted, then shots rang out.

It was a ghastly sight. A dozen defenceless women lying on the ground dead, or seriously wounded, simply because in their compassion they had tried to give us water to ease our thirst. As we shuffled on, we raised caps in silent homage to these latest victims of German brutality.

They hustled us out of town and into a large field for the night. We were told the Germans regretted they could provide no food, but they hoped to have something the next day. When they ringed us with bright lights, we saw a small stream, towards which we edged for a drink and wash. But the well-equipped French undid their packs, took out their rations, ate well, repacked food, undid their blankets, then settled down in comfort for the night. *We* had nothing to eat: we slept in what clothes we had. Around midnight it rained heavily, but what could we do? I pulled my greatcoat up further over my head and slept fitfully.

Next morning at 6 a.m. they woke us by firing their rifles over us. All shot up from sodden beds. On one side I was dry, but on the other side soaked. The French folded blankets which now, being wet, would be heavier to carry, we thought with satisfaction. Then they hastily ate a snack while we stood around tongues hanging out. The Germans relished the scene. They seemed to have had orders to turn the French against the English: they did this task with zeal.

This time the French marched in front, for they had complained we went too fast for them. Just before we started, three English and a French soldier were hauled up. "These men have been caught in the town trying to escape," said the officer-in-charge. "They will be punished now!" The English were taken to one side, a German firing squad lined up and fired. Before our horrified eyes the three slumped to the ground dead. Then they led the Frenchman forward. The officer whispered to a corporal who walked to the man, shouted at him, then punched his face and body. He took a bashing before he fell to the ground, and it was minutes before he could stagger up to rejoin his comrades. But he was alive. The Germans felt safe in shooting any of us, for our records were not yet taken, and any man not reported later as a P.O.W. would be presumed killed in action.

We took the road again. As the sun got hotter and hotter my feet ached more and more. My wound was festering, but I dared not take my boots off at night lest they be stolen by those without boots. It was fatal to drop out by the roadside, for the Germans used their rifle butts viciously. Already that morning we heard shots, and news spread down the line that any straggler who could *not* go on was shot and already we had seen a dozen hit by passing trucks.

At noon, after five-and-a-half hours under scorching sun, we were told we could rest and use the next field as a latrine. Then we heard shots again; three fellows were heading for near-by woods. More shots rang out, and only one was left running. The Germans seemed pleased with their bag.

When we moved on my foot was more painful and more swollen. I was tempted to dump my greatcoat, but remembering we would be likely to sleep in the open for some days yet, I kept it. The German guards too seemed browned off with marching and cursed louder than ever. As we passed through villages they would break into houses. If the doors were locked they smashed them down with rifle butts. It was bikes they wanted, and soon most were mounted, grinning at our discomfort and urging us on towards their own rations. Hoping for some food ourselves we tried to step out, but the French with cumbersome packs were in no hurry. They lingered on their native soil. But it meant the English in the middle of the column were sandwiched and crushed and abused by the Germans.

One incident sickened me. A young boy ahead of me bent down to lace his boot. Instantly a German was on to him, and thrust the bayonet up his arse and out his side. He was stretched out on the road as we went by: the agony on his face haunts me still.

Near Frevant our pace increased almost to a gallop. The French had smelt hot food. We could see steaming soup coppers stretched across the road. The Germans had made French women cook us a meal. With our empty stomachs, it seemed the French, who were first there, would never finish. Then we realized with dismay that each Frog had his mess-tin while most of us had no receptacles to fill. We frantically searched for any old tin—sardine or cigarette. Since the ration was "one tin only" the smaller the tin the smaller the ration. After three days it was a cupful or less of potato soup. But others like myself were even worse off, for there were still a hundred men in front of us, and the coppers ran dry. Germans showed some compassion and let us have a cup of so-called coffee and a slice of black bread. But it was mouldy and on our famished stomachs caused violent vomiting. Behind me was very ugly talk, for those there felt the French should have let us too receive some soup.

We again slept in the field; no lights this time, but the Germans had a full guard ringing us. Many men, restless through hunger and marching, instead of sleeping went prowling. Now the French made a cardinal mistake. Not satisfied with their soup ration, they again undid their packed ration. In a moment the prowlers rushed in and seized these meagre reserves. It was all quickly over. Peace was again shattered in another corner when one Englishman crept up to the German ration truck undetected and helped himself. Then another bunch, repeating the act, was caught. Shots rang out and three were lightly wounded, but in the darkness they crawled away unidentified. I lay awake, my foot aching and my stomach heaving against the mouldy bread. I tried thinking of home, of Nan and Marion, but it only made me feel more crushed. There seemed no hope that I could ever see them again. My courage had gone: I felt I could not continue. I was ready to die and prayed that this agony would go. From sheer exhaustion I fell asleep.

With a start I awoke to find someone trying to unstrap my pack from my back. I hit hard and heard a grunt, then jumped up; but in the dark he escaped.

Next day there was talk of what happened that night. Twenty black eyes and scratched faces told their own story. Two men told me their boots had been ripped off them. Others lost their packs which they had used as pillows. Three were badly injured, victims of robbery with violence. We were indeed seeing life in the raw. Our dangers had doubled—maniacal Germans by day and frantic starved troops by night.

Before we left the Kommandant addressed us. He told us we were the scum of the earth, rogues, vagabonds, scoundrels; and when we reached his beloved Vaterland, the Führer had his own way of making us good citizens in his Reich. Because we had stolen German rations, there would be no issue of bread and sausage that morning, *Heil Hitler*. But since it was Saturday, we would march just fifteen miles to Doullens, where we would stay in comfort for the weekend.

Once more the sun beat down. But for the hope of a weekend rest I'd have given up. By early afternoon we were in Doullens, under strict German control. It was badly bombed and the people were cowed.

Our weekend castle was a disused prison, filthy, the stench paralysing. Those ahead had all the cosy cells and floor space. The latrines were unable to take 3,000 men, so most used the small grass courtyards outside. Where else could we go? We waited for food. They said we were too late: there would be none till dawn.

I was surprised to find many Arabs there, captured as crew on British ships. They had all the bunks in the old wardroom. Soon our toughs aggressively demanded those bunks. When the Arabs bluntly refused, fighting broke out and knives flashed. With no defence the attackers withdrew; but the uproar started again on a balcony two storeys up. With a shout, two bodies hurtled down locked together. I turned away sick at heart. Surely somewhere I could find one clean spot on the grass outside.

For the first time in days I took my boots off. Relief surged down to my raw foot. With plenty of water about I now bathed it and dressed it again. But where to sleep? There was not enough grass to stretch straight out. We slept sitting up, and during the night woke to find our necks and limbs stiff and rats scuffling over us.

At dawn they gave us cheese, black bread, and a cup of ersatz coffee to last until dusk. My heaving stomach barely welcomed the food. The miserable day dragged on; the heat increased; the stench rose higher.

Inside the bedlam of free fighting continued unabated. To take our minds off our vile existence I organized an open-air service; almost two hundred came. With tears in our eyes we sang, "Lead, kindly Light, amid the encircling gloom . . . The night is dark, and I am far from home. . . ." Several times, while conducting the service, I was almost too overcome to say the prayers.

On Monday morning I was stiff in every joint. A sharp pain grabbed the centre of my back; but my foot was better. They gave us a little bread and sent us on the road without any speeches. At noon we could rest, but only in a potato and turnip field. When we left it seemed that locusts had stripped it bare. French farmers protested, but who cared? Even the guards did nothing. This gave us more courage; some made audacious raids on deserted homes. These had to be quick for the guards still used their rifles.

But as the days passed, the Germans forgot to give us food. We lived as best we could on raw potatoes and anything else we could grab. By day we cursed the torrid weather and blessed it by night, sleeping under the stars.

As we neared Das Vaterland, our treatment worsened. Each day they made us march longer.

From Fencquillers to Cambrai—nearly thirty miles—was not much when fit, but we were weak, half starved and ill. And above all we were almost broken in spirit; yet when the Germans thought they had us down, some Cockney, Geordie or Scot would raise a laugh that revived us all.

At Cambrai, on 5th June, a week after capture, we lay in a field near the railway station when an air raid started. Though the Germans had said all the English forces had left France, the planes were British. Bombs landed near by— close enough to make our guards run for shelter, leaving us in the open field. But that was the last resistance we saw anywhere.

At Ligny we crossed into Belgium, now fully Hitlerized. As we passed all Belgians kept indoors. Then German supplies began catching up with the German troops and we too received daily rations—usually equal to a single meal, but enough to keep us going though we were still desperately hungry. The Belgian fields suffered like the French; the Germans again killed several for pillaging. We had all reached the stage of being willing to risk our lives for the chance of food.

On 9th June, when in Bastogne, the English P.O.W.s were roused at 5 a.m. while the French slept on. They gave us rations and told us we would walk to Germany. By 11 o'clock we crossed into Luxembourg, the sun still relentlessly beating down. Just after midday they let us rest for half an hour, then marched us on till 3 a.m. when we reached Trier in Germany.

My knees sagged under me; my eyes were blinded by dirt and sweat. In the inevitable field they told us to take a two-hour rest, and *that* after a sixty-five-mile walk on one piece of black bread and some sausage. Then they led us across town for dispersal to all parts of Germany. All Trier turned out to greet us. They cursed and spat on us. They punched us in the face. For an hour we ran that gauntlet. They said we've never leave the Reich alive. Our reception confirmed their claim.

In the camp were hundreds of British P.O.W.s, officers among them. The officers said they had come part-way on lorries. Some of the others had been lucky enough to come by train from Cambrai to Givet. Beside us they were fairly clean. There was a medical room and a field hospital where each of us was examined. As soon as the medical officer saw my foot they whisked me into hospital. For the first time in two weeks, I slept on a bed, even though it was just wooden boards and a straw sack. After I had washed and shaved they lanced my foot and dressed it. Soon they gave us special rations—potato soup and a whole round of bread. How I slept!

The Germans came round hunting malingerers, but it was good to hear our M.O.s stand fast, insisting they were protected by the Geneva Convention. The Germans laughed, saying they couldn't care less about the convention—as we soon found out.

I stayed in hospital till the evening when the Germans had me pack, ready for a train journey next morning. I pointed to my heavily bound foot. How could I get my boot on? The German said, "It won't matter: you'll be on the train for two days. You're going to a Stalag, and you'll then go out to work whether your foot is bad or not," he laughed. "You're a slave now!"

Next morning they gave us a two-day ration. Again we ran the hostile gauntlet to Trier station, and were herded on to a platform. We looked for a carriage: we saw cattle trucks. They bayoneted us in, fifty to a truck, and closed and barred the doors. Two guards were with us. A half-day later we asked to get out. They said the trucks would *not* be opened till we reached our destination.

For the next two days, we had to eat, sleep and do everything else in this awful enclosed truck. Several men with diarrhoea relieved themselves as best they could. The stench was unbelievable, but the Germans showed no sympathy. They could relieve themselves at practically every station.

On the second day, when four collapsed, they were hauled away. On the morning of the third day, the guards flung open the doors and ordered us out. We reeled against fresh air and light; and fell to the ground through sheer exhaustion. The Nazi officer who met us inspected the trucks; he stormed at us and then detailed some to clean them out. Our way was a four-mile march through a forest: no hills, yet it was bliss to be able to see and feel the sun.

The Stalag guards were as tough as any we had yet met, but they were more willing to talk. They said we'd have comfortable beds and plenty of food. They repeated that if we worked, we'd have nothing to fear. Once Britain surrendered we'd stay on as slave workers, while they—the guards—went to England, and claimed our wives and sweethearts for themselves.

I again looked at Fred Neeve dozing in the corner of the cattle truck now taking us to Blechhammer. Not for the first time I felt England *could* be beaten. Yet somehow something always seemed to come and turn the tide. In Fred I had found a friend who could help me along the dangerous path I quietly planned.

# 3

# *Radio in the Germans' Bathroom*

After Lamsdorf's filth and crowds Blechhammer—Arbeits Kommando E/3—seemed a haven. Though on the main road, the camp was hidden behind massive pine trees. Before the war it had been a Hitler Youth Camp. A barbed-wire fence was all they needed to make it into a home for slaves, for the perimeter lights were already there to help Hitler youth publicity. On one side ran the Adolf Hitler Canal from Gleiwitz out east to the Oder River, a few miles west. On the other three sides ran narrow paths for guards to patrol between high sentry boxes at the four corners. There were five large huts, each divided into six rooms. Each room held twelve double-decker beds and a round stove with a long metal stove-pipe going out through the roof. The daily ration of coal per room was one normal-sized bucket that gave us two hours' heat. The German offices for the Kommandant and Paymaster, and quarters for guards, were by the gate just beyond the barbed wire.

A young sergeant from Manchester—Arthur Edge—who spoke good German, acted as camp leader and interpreter, a job which earned him more kicks than praise. But he was certainly helping the men. Already there were 300 P.O.W.s in the camp and, with our 300, all beds were filled.

"It's damned hard work out on the Baustelle [building site]," he told us. "The ground's being cleared for a huge factory to make petrol from coal and our men are digging out tree roots and laying roads. The guards work us like niggers, and right now they're on top."

"Is food any better here than at Lamsdorf?" I asked.

"Yes, there's a reasonable meal when you get back at night, and a ration of bread, ersatz butter, cheese or sausage to take to work. How long it will last no one knows—the Jerries say so long as we work well for the Reich we'll be decently treated. But that doesn't stop them manhandling prisoners on the job. They nearly clouted me twice simply because I translated something for one of the others." He hated the Germans.

Up the road, he said, was a camp for Polish civilians and they were being treated worse than dogs, forbidden even to speak their own language in the presence of a German. But they did their best to help the English P.O.W.s, with a packet of cigarettes or a loaf of bread finding its way into our camp from this source. If caught, the Germans mercilessly beat them.

That evening we ate a bowl of soup with real meat in it, the first we'd tasted since being captured. Even if it had been horse it would have tasted good. Dead beat we fell asleep straight away.

The Germans roused us at 4.30 a.m. Guards rushed into our rooms prodding with a sharp bayonet anyone who wasn't already up. Fred and I were bundled into a party of thirty men and marched a mile and a half to the Baustelle.

Loading huge cobblestones on to a lorry was hard on hands unused to manual labour. If we paused for breath the guard reminded us with his rifle butt that we were working for his Führer: he would have no slacking. But when he tried to give us fresh orders we all pretended not to know a word of German and deliberately misinterpreted his signs. This maddened him.

After two days he called me over and waved his arms while I stood dumb before him. I let him repeat the motion several times, then appeared to understand what he was getting at. I was to become party foreman. That suited me of course, for it gave me freedom to move around and keep my eyes open; but I wanted to avoid bad feeling with Fred Neeve and another sergeant in our party. I tried to point this out to the guard but he wouldn't listen. How could a man who had only a small crown on his forearm be of higher rank than one who had three stripes, a gun and crown? No, I was obviously of much higher rank, and therefore must be foreman. The difficulty was resolved a few days later when they split our party into three. The two other sergeant-majors became foremen of the other groups.

In my group was a man called Reg Beattie. From the first he struck me as a true blue Tory. He hated the guts of every

German and was always in trouble with the guard because he simply refused to work. We found much in common for he came from Brighton, which before the war had been my second home. His view was that we wouldn't be P.O.W.s much longer: within a few weeks the Allies would knock hell out of the Germans.

"But how can we knock hell out of 'em when France is finished and the B.E.F. has fled home?" I objected.

"The trouble with you is that you listen too much to the bloody Jerry propaganda. I've been speaking to some Froggy P.O.W.s this morning, and they say the Germans are being driven back on all fronts. German morale is low. It's all lies about the fall of Paris."

"Well, I believe France *is* out of the war, and what's more that we'll be prisoners for another five years. It'll take that long to get the Nazis out of the occupied countries."

Reg and I often crossed swords in arguments, and I noticed that the rest of the men began to regard me as a little pro-German too. I had been considering how best to carry out my orders to get information to England, and it struck me as a good idea to let the Germans think I was in sympathy with them. And so I went out of my way to get on the right side of the guards. My own room-mates and fellow workers became more and more suspicious of me, especially when I started asking Arthur Edge to translate messages to the Kommandant which indicated that I wanted to win German favour. And so the feeling that I was anti-British spread through the camp. It was important that it should, for it would be a waste of time kidding the Germans unless my own men were deceived too.

The Germans had a nasty habit of putting their own English-speaking men in our midst in English uniforms to act as spies and I knew that if the slightest whisper of my work got abroad it would be quickly back to them.

Having gained the confidence of the guards, and as foreman of the group, I was now free to wander round the huge site. I made a careful study of the works which was rapidly going up, and found where the vital points were.

There was other important work to prepare for. As time went on our men in sheer despair would obviously try to escape. Could one not create links from one part of Germany to another, and then from one country to another? Around

John Brown; a photograph taken at Lamsdorf and sent home to his wife.

Prince Waldemar Hohenlohe, the humane Blechhammer Camp Kommandant. Related to the British royal family, and transferred to Italy by the Nazis for being too lenient with the British prisoners, he in turn became a prisoner of the British. After the war he and John Brown kept in touch for several years.

us on the work site was a rare mixture of foreign workers, most treated as slaves, and I set out to contact as many of them as possible. Merely to be seen talking to another foreigner was dangerous, and there was always the risk that the fellow would run to the Germans with information in return for more bread. But my luck held and slowly I made good contacts. I discovered that although Hitler was outwardly master of Europe, a powerful fifth column was forming underground in every conquered nation. Escape routes were worked out and addresses obtained; but it still seemed that it would be hazardous to get out of Germany.

Some of my contacts were willing to change places with British P.O.W.s, so that the prisoner could escape more easily while the foreigner gained the protection of the English camp. Such things as radios, cameras and civilian clothing were strictly forbidden in all camps, and the penalty for possessing any was death. But we needed a radio badly for B.B.C. official news from England before we all went crazy at the absurd rumours and German claims. I was anxious also to get a good camera as I knew any photographs of ill-treatment could be valuable evidence in any post-war enquiries. Without civilian clothing escapes would be well nigh impossible. It would be no easy matter to get these things because of the stringent searching each P.O.W. had on return to camp at night; but the risk would have to be taken.

And so those first three months at Blechhammer were spent preparing for the future. It was up to me to match my intelligence against that of the Germans. If I did not get away with it, then that would be just too bad.

One day we were marching to the Baustelle our guard took out his wallet and handed me photographs, the most disgusting I'd ever seen; but he doubtless thought they would compensate for our enforced celibacy. I gave them back and made it quite clear we were not interested in porn. He laughed and said, "Very soon we'll all be landing in England and then I'll be sleeping like this with your wives while you work on here for the Reich."

For the next few days he went among the P.O.W.s repeating his threat of abusing our wives; he was always finding fault and using his rifle butt; we all loathed him. Soon after, when he was changed to another working party unloading coal from steel railway trucks, whose sides dropped outwards to let coal fall down, his reputation had gone before him. This day he was shouting at one man whom he accused of slacking, and striding towards him beside the truck, rifle menacingly raised. Then the coal truck opened, and nearly ten tons landed on him. He was a mess when they shovelled him clear; but the men could establish beyond all doubt that his death was an accident. Life had taught us to be ruthless; and the more brutal the Germans became, the more intense became our desire for revenge.

Our E/3 cookhouse was yet not ready for use. All meals were prepared in the Polish canteen a quarter of a mile away. Every Sunday morning forty of us would go there to peel potatoes. With no news from home the men were becoming increasingly depressed; and to encourage them a little we organized community hymn singing while we peeled potatoes. Even the toughest would quietly wipe a tear from the corner of his eyes.

One Sunday the German Fräulein in charge of the canteen beckoned me over. She handed me food and cigarettes, and indicated she would be seeing me again as she walked home to Ehrenforst along the path beside the canal that led past my hut. She next started passing us as we marched out to work, handing me a parcel. Because I was giving him English lessons the guard on duty at this time would wink, and if he thought the parcel would be found on me, he would carry it into the camp for me. Sometimes it was cigarettes or cake and butter, or even a bottle of wine.

I began to feel awkward at receiving so much when I could give nothing in return. I asked Arthur Edge to thank her and find out if I could repay her in any way. When he came back with his blunt answer, I blushed. "She says she wants to have a baby by you!" Fortunately for my peace of mind she was soon transferred to another part of the Baustelle. But even though we did not meet, regular parcels still came.

One day in early September the camp Kommandant sent for me to tell me that in future I would not go out to work: I would join camp staff, form a library, run the canteen and perhaps later help with camp entertainment. At first I thought my activities with the foreign workers had been found out, or else the fact that I was receiving parcels from the German girl. But it seemed that the guard, thinking he was doing me a good turn to give me a camp staff job, had told the Kommandant about my friendly attitude. In fact it was a bitter blow, after all the preparations, for I felt I'd lose all my links with the outside and be unable to carry on my special task. But I could not refuse without arousing suspicion.

A few days later we were told we were to return to Lamsdorf while the camp was being de-loused. This was much needed, but I did not want to leave Blechhammer and, when I found that a small party would remain de-lousing the rooms, I managed to join it. It took three days: all bedding was burned: every bed and board scrubbed. Our own clothes went through a barrel-type de-louser while we scrubbed ourselves outside.

The men returning from Lamsdorf marched down the road singing "Roll out the Barrel", and with them was an accordion—our first musical instrument. There were new faces including C.S.M. Haberfield and C.S.M. Jack Hobbs. They would be in charge and run the camp from Room 3 (*Stube Drei*).

I became camp clerk, counting the working parties each day. There was no morning roll call, the total number being checked by adding the number leaving on each party against sick who remained in camp. It was easy to confuse the Germans who seemed unable to count except in fives, and even then rarely got the right answer. Fred Neeve, Arthur Edge and I were inclined to stay in our own room near the Adolf Hitler Canal. But the splitting-up of camp staff was too much for the Germans who could never find any of us when they wanted us. So we three were moved into Room 3. We five N.C.O.s decided to pool our food and mess together. *Stube Drei* began in late September.

Because Arthur Edge and I were not "regular Army" we had to listen to long tirades about our ignorance on all matters military. Arthur, the youngest, was just twenty-one when captured; and he had learnt German while working in a Manchester office after graduating from the university. The Germans called him "Der Artur", the British "Otto", and the name stuck.

C.S.M. Haberfield—'Haber" to all—who came from

Bristol, had been in the Glosters since the First World War and took charge of the camp. C.S.M. Jack Hobbs from Ashington also belonged to the Glosters. A talented musician, he had been sergeant-major when war started. Later another quartermaster was called in to deal with clothing: C.Q.M.S. Riley, known as Moggy, London born, had been in the Rifle Brigade for seventeen years.

From the first there was friction between us all, mainly because of my apparent friendliness with the Germans. But we decided to sink personal differences and do all we could together to help the men. When later I began to get supplies into the canteen they began to realize that perhaps after all I was working for the good of the camp.

But daily the men were getting more depressed. After four months as P.O.W.s there were still no letters from England, though we heard that the Stalags were now getting mail and Red Cross food parcels. The German news, which we had to hear from the camp loudspeaker, was grim. Preceded by a fanfare of trumpets, their "Special Reports" always meant details of devastating air raids on England, of ships sunk, or of the huge armada about to be launched into the English Channel.

One morning in a German newspaper I read that an important port called Sunbury-on-Thames had been bombed. At first I roared with laughter that dear old sleepy Sunbury was an important port; but I soon sobered up. They had at least named the place, and there seemed no reason to doubt that it had been bombed. I began to fear that my home and family had gone in the raid, and I vowed to redouble efforts to get information to England. If I had already lost all it would hardly matter if I lost my life as well.

At this time I began sending off messages to England. One contact on the Baustelle—a Dutch civilian—could get letters to England through a sea-captain sailing from Stetten to Sweden. The letters, addressed to my wife, or sometimes fictitious relatives, contained messages in code* for M.I.6

*For exact details of how the letter code worked see *M.I.9—The British Secret Service That Fostered Escape and Evasion 1939–45 and Its American Counterpart* by M. R. D. Foot and J. M. Langley (Bodley Head, 1979), p. 54: "With the help of a Foreign Office expert called Hooker, Winterbottom and his colleagues developed a code called HK through which several people were communicating with London from Germany who would intercept them. I first sent details about the plant, the Oberschlesischehydrierwerké. Despite my misgivings on joining camp staff I now found there was even more information to send, for I could get about seeking canteen goods not only in Ehrenforst—the nearest village— but even to cities such as Gleiwitz or Breslau. On the way to the village I would pass other Baustellen, which indicated new works of immense importance to the German war effort. I was certainly worried for, with no mail coming in, I did not know if my messages had got through to London.

As the German news improved, our P.O.W. treatment worsened, and we could not put forward our complaints as we had seen no member of the Protecting Power. The men were forced to work, however bad the weather, and when they came in at night, drenched and exhausted, there were no clothes driers. The Germans said we needed no coal till winter. Then we had no doctor and some were badly injured, either by the guards or at work.

The food shortage became so acute that rations were stolen in the barrack rooms: we had to police soup lines because several tried to get a double helping. The climax came one night when the Germans discovered their bread store had been broken into. Guards rushed into our rooms and forced us all to get out of bed and parade in night attire in the bitter cold outside. Then the Kommandant screamed and demanded that the culprits stand forward. Until they did the whole camp would stand out in the cold, all night if need be, then go out to work as always in the morning. No one stirred: we stood for an hour in the icy wind. The guards in uniform cursed that they too had to face the cold with

---

by November 1940. . . . Like several codes developed later, HK was at once fairly simple to use, and in skilled hands unusually hard to detect. All the user had to do was to indicate by the fashion in which he wrote the date that the letter contained a message, showing by his opening words which part of the code he was using, and then writing an apparently normal chatty letter, from which the inner meaning could be unravelled with the code's help." On pp. 322–4 there is a specimen message set out. See also *From Colditz in Code* by J. M. Green (Robert Hale, 1971), pp. 161–86, for full details on how to decode the letters. One can see how clearly they were written and how impossible it was for an outsider to know that a message lay within them.

us—but at least they were properly dressed. Then a German Gefreiter (corporal) discovered footprints leading from the bread store down to a room near the canal. The Kommandant said that unless the actual criminal confessed every member of that room would have a week's solitary confinement and no food. This was too much for the poor devils who had stolen the bread. To save their comrades they stepped forward.

The Kommandant gave an order. Six men were led to a spot in the woods nearby in a circle of light. The guards raised their rifles and fired. But as the smoke cleared the men were still standing, unhurt. Then the Kommandant gave a further order. "This time fire to kill!" Once again the rifles blazed—and once again we saw to our amazement that the men were still on their feet, bewildered and chalky white. The Kommandant and guards roared with laughter. The whole thing had been arranged to teach us a lesson and frighten out of their wits the half-starved fellows who, from sheer hungry, had been driven to steal. But this was not the end of the incident. The Kommandant next called for all members of Room 3 to step forward. We had to stand and watch while the guards brutally bashed the prisoners in the face, chest and stomach. Not a cry escaped the men and when they were barely able to stand they were handed over to us, the Kommandant remarking, "Let that be a lesson to the whole camp. In future we'll show no mercy whatever to any of you. *Gute nacht: Schlafen Sie wohl* (Good night: Sleep well)!"

This incident can be said to be the nadir of our time at Blechhammer, for if things at times seemed bad, they never were as bad again.

To start with, 23rd September was a red-letter day for seven men in the camp: two letters and five parcels came from England. This caused great excitement, and the letters were passed around for all to read. Because of censorship there was little war news in them, but one had a sense of determination to battle on whatever the cost. They improved camp morale. The Germans were astounded by our buoyancy. It was almost as though we had been living in a lost world since capture, and now at last were relinked with civilization.

And the very next day a parcel arrived for me. As I came

through the gates tightly clutching it, the men surged forward: I was left in no doubt what a lucky devil I was. Nobody in Room 3 said a word while I opened it and took out coffee, tea, cheese, butter, chocolate, meat roll and English cigarettes.

"What about mucking in on this parcel, and when one of you gets one, we can do the same again?" I said.

"That's all right, Busty—it's your parcel: keep it for yourself."

But with a little persuasion they agreed to share, and that night we had something like a real English supper, ending with a cup of tea—the most delectable drink we had ever tasted. The leaves were kept for the next brew because we intended to spin out the little packet for as long as possible. In *Stube Drei* we somehow had more visits than usual for the next few days—somehow whenever we were brewing up, and few were sent away. I never found out who sent that parcel.

Later my wife confirmed it did *not* come from her. But two days later, when I was lighting the fire with the paper wrapping, I noticed two pieces had been stuck together. I carefully peeled them apart, and on one side saw faint and legible writing. My eyes nearly popped from my head as I read it through. I called Fred over: and when he had finished reading I saw him brush a tear from his eye.

It was from that historic speech of Churchill. "Even though large tracts of Europe and famous states have fallen or may fall into the grip of the Gestapo, and all the odious apparatus of Nazi rule, we shall not flag or fail. We shall go on to the end; we shall fight . . . on the seas and oceans; we shall fight with growing confidence and growing strength in the air; we shall defend our island whatever the cost may be. We shall fight on the beaches; we shall fight on the landing grounds; we shall fight in the fields and in the streets; we shall fight in the hills. We shall *never surrender*." Underneath was written: "The Prime Minister said this over the B.B.C. on 4th June 1940." Now we knew why the Germans hated Churchill so much.

It was essential that every man in the camp should receive this message from his leader. That night we feverishly made fifty copies—one per room. From then on the Germans, though they tried every possible ruse from brutality to cunning, were never again on top. And as time went on and with Red Cross and food parcels arriving, we took every opportunity at Jerry baiting.

It was clear that we were missing B.B.C. news. We ought to be sure of hearing speeches like this, not only to encourage our own men, but also the slave workers on the Baustelle. I had already organized to buy a radio, but the stumbling block was how to get it into E/3. Meanwhile I asked Fred Neeve: "If I could get a radio from outside would you be willing to operate it?"

"Of course I would," he replied, "and if needed could transcribe Morse messages."

"Do you realize that if you're caught, the Germans would bump you off on the spot?"

"So what? So long as I have a job to do I couldn't care less. Have you thought about the place to operate the set?"

"It would be right under the Jerries' noses. Their bathroom is on our side of the wire, and we could use the little room at the back where our own bath orderly sleeps to service it for them."

"That would mean operating it with earphones, but it's far safer that way."

We agreed to tell no one until I found how to get it past the guards at the gates. It was just after this that I received a most heartening message. In a letter from a pretended relative M.I.6 conveyed to me that my messages were reaching them and being put to good use; they asked me to send as much as possible. It was what they needed and made all my worry worthwhile. So when a good postal link, through the Red Cross, was established after Dunkirk I was able to send even more letters home. A private of the line was allowed two postcards and one letter card a month and no more, but since I had official business I had access to as many forms as I liked.

About that time the tide unexpectedly turned even more in our favour. The old Kommandant went from Blechhammer and in his place came Waldemar, Prince of Hohenlohe Oehringen.

I was standing looking at the camp notice board one day when I heard a very cultured voice say in perfect English: "Who is responsible for these notices on the board?" I turned around and saw the Prince in his beautifully cut uniform, leaning on a walking stick (he had a stiff leg from a First World War injury).

"They are put up by the camp sergeant-major," I replied.

"His spelling is a little faulty, and shall we say his grammar is a little faulty too?" He pointed to a sentence which was admittedly not perfect, but would certainly have passed with most P.O.W.s. I was abashed to hear a foreigner so critical.

"Are the prisoners fairly comfortable in the camp, and is the food as good as can be expected?" the Prince continued.

Recovering from my surprise I took the opportunity of mentioning various points. The rooms were overcrowded. We had no concert hall. We were very short of library books and we needed a medical officer and camp hospital where patients could be treated. The food was *not* as good as when we first came and Red Cross parcels were not coming in as they should. The Prince promised to look into all these matters and do his utmost to make our life more tolerable.

When I reported this conversation in Room 3 we all laughed at the sergeant-major over his grammar and spelling; but for the rest they would not believe me and accused me of fraternizing with the enemy. It was then that I decided to go all out for an apparent friendship with the Germans. For a start it seemed the best way to secure much-needed improvements in the camp.

A few days later the Prince sent for me and not only handed me eighty books which came from Lamsdorf, but augmented this stock with some from his own collection. We were thus able to start a library which was widely used. Soon after this we organized concerts; but these had to be given in one of the rooms that could hold no more than thirty. But it was a start to camp life.

By then the men had many contacts with civilian workers outside, and each night many smuggled in bread or eggs or any other food they had bartered for. Then the Germans would make a sudden search, and a table be piled high with all contraband. We heard rumours of more stringent nightly searches: unless we moved quickly the chance to get a radio would be lost for ever.

In late October I again contacted the man who was willing

to supply it for several hundred marks* and the promise of food when our parcels came from England. He was a German worker who hated the Nazis and was also involved with us on other fiddles. I arranged with him to bring the set one day to one of us and fix the deal. Our problem was to find a man willing to take the risk, for all knew that to be caught with a radio was a safe pass into the next world. It had to be someone who worked near the canteen, for suspicion would at once be aroused if a prisoner wandered too far from his own party. Fred and I decided on a man from a nearby party and sent for him. "Would you be willing to do something that would greatly help the camp."

"Of course, if it's at all within my power."

"We've bought a radio outside and want you to bring it into E/3. The German civilian who is near you on the job is our contact, and it must be done tomorrow night without fail."

"This sounds very simple. Leave it to me and you'll have it at 5 p.m. tomorrow."

He was a quiet type and unlikely to talk about the grave danger he was deliberately walking into; but all the same his calmness surprised us a little, and in the morning our prayers went with him. The day dragged on, we could not settle down to any work: we feared we'd sent a man to his doom.

At 4.30 p.m. we went to the canteen where we could watch the parties coming in. When the first bunch arrived, our worst fears were confirmed. The Germans made a thorough search of every man, confiscating everything except bundles of old firewood. It was the first complete search they'd held and the results were astonishing: potatoes, bread, marge and even meat lay piled high on the table. Then the party with our man arrived at the gates, and what we saw shook us.

"My God, Fred, he's got the damned thing strapped to his back!"

---

* The basis of all trade and acquisition of marks was barter. The key items were cigarettes, tea, chocolate, soap and coffee. The French supplied French cigarettes, "Sweet Caporal", which were available to P.O.W.s through camp canteens at thirty francs for a packet of twenty. One of these packets could be sold for five marks to the Germans and, later, for ten marks—Reichmarks not Lagermarks. There was never any difficulty in getting Reichmarks in a camp like Blechhammer.

"You said it would be a small set. Looks like a bloody pantechnicon," Fred replied anxiously.

We watched frightened and fascinated as the Germans searched each prisoner. We could hardly bear to look when it came to our man. They turned out his pockets, felt all down his body, looked in his rucksack and turned down his socks. Then they let him go. The impossible had happened; they had reasoned the package was far too big to be anything *verboten* and was likely some job he'd brought in to repair for one of the Nazis bosses on the Baustelle.

When he later slipped the set into Room 3 we thanked him and asked what had made him do it that way.

"Well," he replied, "I tried to get the chap next to me to help carry it in; but he wasn't keen so I had to carry it on my own. No trouble at all: though big it isn't heavy."

"But don't you think you were taking a terrific risk doing it so openly?"

"Risk of what?"

At first we thought he was pulling our leg, but it became clear he hadn't the least idea of the enormous risk he had taken.

That night Fred listened to the B.B.C. news in the bathroom, and when he came back he sat down on his bed. "Gather round chaps, I've got something that might interest you." Fred slowly read the bulletin, and when it was over there was an uncanny silence. I knew the questions now racing through our minds. This bulletin sounded factual and genuine after the hysterical German news.

Then Otto broke the silence. "That's B.B.C. news. Where the devil did you get it from?"

"We've got a radio in the camp."

"I don't believe you—it's bloody impossible to get one past the Jerries the way they're searching now."

We then told them how we got the set: for security reasons no one would see it, nor would we say where it was.

Night after night Fred listened and put out bulletins which were sent to the foreign prisoners and slave workers on the Baustelle. They now treated the German news as a joke, and if a guard tried to say the war was almost over, *"Deutschland über Alles"*, they laughed him down and gave our version. The Germans angrily determined to find the source of our news. Surrounding camps were searched but nothing was found. One day the Prince sent for me and said the authorities suspected there was a radio in E/3.

"But that's impossible: how could we get one in?"

"That is something we do not know; but there is no doubt that B.B.C. news bulletins are being circulated at the works, and one of the British P.O.W.s has told a guard that the news comes from E/3."

"I can assure you there could not be a set in any of our rooms, otherwise I would certainly know about it." I was speaking the truth, for the German bathroom was not one of ours: we were in fact forbidden to use the washing facilities there.

"Well, I warn you that if the bulletins continue, the whole camp will be searched."

We had two sets of earphones. One night, when I was listening with Fred, there was a knock at the door. Quickly we hid the set and earphones under some blankets, picked up books and with hearts beating fast opened the door. A little German guard with a towel over his arm, who had just showered, walked in, looking surprised at us and said nothing. He looked under the table and in all corners of the room. He moved the blankets and then said, "Sorry to disturb you but can one of you give me a match?" We could not believe our luck: so near to discovery and all for a match. I quickly gave one to him and a packet of cigarettes as well.

Fred mopped his brow. "We'll not be so lucky next time. Do you think he spotted something but decided to say nothing while we were here?"

"I don't think any Jerry could keep quiet in such circumstances, but we can't carry on operating the set from here. How about putting it in the carpenter's shop. Jim Hurley could hide it for us there."

Shortly after, one quiet Sunday morning, forty Brownshirts entered the camp, under the direction of the German Paymaster, Zahlmeister Brauner. They pulled the place to pieces, even stripping the wooden walls down and looking in the roof. There had been no warning of the raid, and when they came to Room 3 I was caught in the act of shaving with an electric razor, which I'd obtained from one of the Dutch civilians. All I could do was to carry on shaving as if nothing was wrong. While the Brownshirts turned everything apart, the Paymaster spotted the wire attached to the razor, pounced on it and examined it carefully. "What is this?" he said.

"It's an electric razor sent to me from England."

"But I've never heard of an electric razor before. Where are they made?"

I took a chance and said, "We used to import them from Holland. They've been used there for some time."

"Ah that's why there's a Dutch trade mark on the side of the box." As he handed the razor back he said laughingly, "I really thought I'd found the radio that time!"

They left the room and went to the carpenter's shop. We followed—hearts in our mouths—hoping we might be able to distract them. The Paymaster sat down in an armchair made from Red Cross boxes, and saw me standing in the doorway. "We've good information that the radio set is in this carpenter's shop, and I don't intend moving from here until we've found it."

The searchers did their best, but found nothing. The Paymaster looked furious as he left the room.

"I wonder if his backside was burning while he was sitting on the chair?" I said to Fred when he'd gone. We both laughed: the set was in the chair.

These were the first of many miraculous escapes for the set. Fred Neeve never failed to produce his daily bulletin which saved so many P.O.W.s from mental breakdown. He continued to carry out his work in a calm and casual manner, the shadow of death often inches from him. For although the Germans never suspected Fred personally, they were for ever on the lookout for the source of the B.B.C. news.

# 4

## *"Deutschland ist Kaputt"*

During October 1940 letters began trickling in from England; but when nothing came from Nan, I became seriously worried. I tried to keep a happy front, and betted with my room-mates I'd have a special treat on my birthday, 15th November. Sure enough in the post that October day came her letter written on 6th September. The War Office had informed her I was missing, believed killed. Then on 6th September she had received both a letter containing her war-widow's pension-book, and the card I'd written from Lamsdorf on 15th June. She said she had always believed I would turn up somewhere. All was well at home, though our local had been bombed besides other familiar landmarks. The letter revived me and I could hardly wait for the next; but that was weeks away.

As the year wore on, the weather grew colder. The first snow fell on 15th October, and on 5th November a severe gale hit the camp: tall pine trees snapped like match-sticks. Many of our men had lucky escapes on the Baustelle when scaffolding came crashing to the ground; but the Germans made the prisoners carry on. Now the temperatures fell much lower. The men went out to work in poor boots and thin clothing with 30 degrees of frost showing on the thermometer. Many were frost bitten. We protested, but the Prince was powerless to help for, work-wise, the camp came under German Civilian Authority—not the Wehrmacht. We asked to see the Protecting Power and further pressed our need for a camp medical officer. At last on 10th December Lieutenant Desmond Cribb R.A.M.C. came to Blechhammer. His arrival heralded a new and better period for us all. From the start he went bullet-headed at the Germans: they soon learned to respect him.

By devious means we began to collect medical instruments for him; but meantime Desmond Cribb carried out minor operations like lancing boils—which were almost epidemic—with a razor blade. The Germans would not allow us to give Cribb a room of his own to sleep in, so Room 3 gained a new inmate. As time went on he was able to keep off work dozens of men who before would have been forced to go out. And if any of the Germans themselves wanted medical treatment—for they too had no local doctor of their own—they had to line up for our sick parade and take their turn with us.

Throughout December the snow lay thick on the ground. The laden pine trees glistened in the brilliant sunlight; the beauty of the scene was lost on P.O.W.s leaving for work. Had it not been for the daily B.B.C. news bulletin life would have indeed been miserable. The Germans were even perkier than ever, assuring us that London was completely flattened and that as soon as the weather improved, they'd be landing in England. But we knew better. The only point on which we differed amongst ourselves was the length of time it would take to finish the Germans off. Most P.O.W.s were quite sure they'd be back in England for the next summer. But I could not forget that damning speech of Chamberlain and his prediction—six years of war.

At times the air in Room 3 boiled.

"You know, Busty, I think I'd rather have one of your stinking farts than this miserable talk of yours."

"I'm not trying to depress you, but why the hell don't you use your common sense?"

"Trouble with you, Busty, you speak without experience of military matters—pity your common sense isn't as strong as your wind. You can't really think the Jerries will win the war?"

"Don't be a bloody fool, you know damn well I don't."

"Then why say you don't think we'll be home for Christmas 1940, let alone summer 1941."

"Simply because I'm sure we're not capable of beating the Jerries before then."

"You've always put the bastards on a pedestal. Why the hell don't you join them if you think so much of them?"

Then Otto in the corner would belch loudly and the vicious battery would switch on him. And so the seven of us lived together, swearing and cursing each other, taking turns to pollute the already insufficient air, and having as our chief subjects of conversation—food, sex, war, religion and home life. That we did not come to blows was simply because there was usually someone sensible enough to intervene at the right moment, and make us laugh at ourselves.

As Christmas drew near, the Germans taunted us at being behind barbed wire instead of celebrating at home. They had plenty of food, but we were getting only occasional Red Cross parcels; and our German daily ration had been cut to a bowl of weak soup and thin bread. Even the ersatz coffee seemed weaker now that the acorn season was over. But try as they would, the Germans could not break our spirit. They at times succeeded with the Poles, French and Jews camped around the Baustelle, but not us.

One incident at this time greatly angered the Germans. Snow lay thick on the ground, and as the first party from E/3 arrived at the work gates, the men saw a large snowman directly in their line of march. The features were those of Winston Churchill complete with his hat and cigar, and all built by the Werkschutz, or Brownshirt Police, in charge of Baustelle security. Nearby shuffled a Jewish working party with a dozen German guards, laughing as they saw the English prisoners advancing. Our men marched in unusual silence. When the Durham Light Infantry corporal in charge drew level with the snowman, he roared, "Party, eyes right!" and every man smartly saluted. The Germans at first were dumbfounded; but then some Jews—poor sods—started to laugh, and the guards turned on them with rifle butts. Meanwhile the Brownshirts demolished the snowman so that no other party had the chance to pay homage to Churchill.

The next morning when the guards came into the camp they saw a life-like snowman of Hitler looking the picture of misery, and around his neck a board saying *"Deutschland Kaputt"*. The Germans saw no joke and stopped our bread ration for the day. But it was worth it especially when we heard that the perimeter guards who had been on duty that night had been severely reprimanded for not catching the culprits red-handed.

Christmas Day 1940 I can never forget. First came a letter

Phil Kirby and Jimmy Newcomb in Blechhammer in 1942. This picture was taken with a camera which the British P.O.W.s had smuggled into the camp.

Captain John Borrie, New
Zealand Medical Corps,
and C.S.M. Haberfield at
Ehrenforst in 1943

A group photograph taken
at Blechhammer: from
left, C.Q.M.S. Riley,
R.S.M. McKenzie, Captain
Warren, Captain Noakes,
C.S.M.Haberfield,
C.S.M. Neave and John
Brown

that morning—a letter that meant more to me than any present I'd ever received. The news from England was cheerful; it was obvious that the first shock of the London bombing had faded. Some of my letters were getting through, and we felt that, separated as we were, at least we could convey our love to each other through the written word. Nan's letter ended hoping the war would be over and that we could have a wonderful Christmas together next year. I prayed to God it would be so; but as long as Nan was there for me, I could not care how long I had to wait.

We held a service in the bath-house. Although the weather was bitterly cold, two hundred came. Desmond Cribb and I shared the conducting of the service, and when we said prayers for our loved ones in danger at home, many wept unashamedly. Christmas dinner was a bowl of barley soup and three potatoes. Because of transport problems from snow there was even less bread than usual, and no Red Cross parcels had come for some time. Room 3 was cheerless, but we attempted to console ourselves with thoughts of pre-war days and after dinner we produced from its hiding place our wine or "Hooch" which had been brewed under the very noses of the Germans. Alcohol was of course strictly forbidden, but we knew that many rooms had made their own brew. Before the war I had worked for Truman's Brewery and had several times been asked, "Busty, how does one brew?"

That night we held an organized concert and, if the Germans thought they'd cowed us by short rations, they soon found otherwise. Our "Christmas cheer" worked, men shouted and sang carols in various corners of E/3. The guards looked on amazed: they knew we had nothing to drink, and certainly very little to make us shout about. And most of us felt Christmas 1940 was a day we could fairly turn our backs on. Conditions could hardly be worse: things could only improve.

But there was a tragic sequel. A Welsh lad Gilderdale suddenly fell seriously ill. Though Desmond and a German doctor gave him every attention, he died within a few hours. The Germans suspected some form of alcohol poisoning, but nothing was proved. After this, it seemed that every man in the camp came to me. We discovered that some were indeed attempting to make spirit from shoe polish or meths. The guards continued regular room searches looking for fermenting vessels. All they saw were German sauerkraut barrels obtained through our canteen.

With the New Year—1941—all generally accepted that their present home had to suffice for some time yet. It did not take long for us to discover the bartering value of tea, chocolate, soap and cigarettes. I needed help with transporting canteen goods bought from the Ehrenforst store owned by Kapitza. Someone had the idea of pinching an E/3 barrow from the Baustelle for me. It had a contractor's name painted on it. When they wheeled it out from the Baustelle the Werkschutz thought all must be well for the guards did not challenge them. But once the barrow was inside E/3 it was scraped down and repainted with Arbeits Kommando E/3 on the side. Gradually other articles left the Baustelle. The Germans thus decided to raid our camp to see if we had their stolen property; but as usual we had been forewarned.

The canteen was proving a most useful asset and as soon as I had any surplus Red Cross goods I began a bartering business, especially for clothing which could be used in helping those who planned to escape. The difficulty was getting the stuff within the camp and spirited away before the prying eyes of the German Paymaster Brauner detected anything. The road into the camp was always in full view of his office. As soon as we went out of camp for goods he would sit watching for our return. He suspected we were bribing the guards, and he wasn't far wrong. My game was to take three men with me to help push the barrow filled with canteen goods back. When he came in view of his office, one of them would go in front to ask the Paymaster to come and check prices with us. He was flattered that we trusted him. While he was checking prices we slipped the goods through. What was not whisked quickly out of sight was slipped into the canteen stove till he came out and made his personal check that everything was in order. We knew he suspected us but he was not clever enough to catch us at it.

As time went on, I realized more and more the importance of these trips to the shops, for I was able to collect some information which would be invaluable for future bombing and which, of course, I sent home.

Meanwhile, some of our men who had gone back sick or

for punishment to Lamsdorf, had let slip about our radio. The Lamsdorf Camp Leader, R.S.M. Sherriff, decided he too wanted one for Stalag use. By devious means a request came back to us, asking us to get them a set, which they would collect. We knew that most men in the Stalag had new uniforms and boots through Red Cross sources, whilst most at Blechhammer were still wearing what they'd been captured in. So I agreed to help Lamsdorf on condition they sent down a full lorry-load of Red Cross clothing. In exchange we would send back some surplus food parcels, making out to the Germans that we had more than enough to go round.

I managed to negotiate another radio and get it into the camp on the canteen truck through the Polish canteen. When the Lamsdorf lorry came with clothing we made the swap and slipped the special parcel in with the others. In Lamsdorf Red Cross food store it was duly issued to R.S.M. Sherriff as his weekly food ration and German security (Abwehr) never knew how.

In April 1941 the war news grew worse: the Germans invaded Greece. Outside E/3 we saw the Silesian roads crowded with army vehicles, tanks, guns, and ammo trucks. At first we assumed it was a general movement for grand scale manoeuvres; but, as the procession continued day and night for over a month, we wondered why. The columns, with accompanying squadrons of planes, were moving towards Poland. Poland was *kaputt*: beyond Poland lay Russia. What could be going on? Though Russia we knew had double-crossed Poland and had made a lasting pact with Germany, this long procession could mean only one thing.

In mid-May I was in Paymaster Brauner's office discussing goods for the canteen and as usual arguing over the quantity of dubbin the old rogue wanted to dump on us before we could buy other goods. Suddenly, for no apparent reason, he looked at the unbroken line of military vehicles passing the window and said, "I suppose those vehicles are going to military manoeuvres to prepare for the invasion of England this summer."

"Far too many guns and tanks have gone by for just an ordinary exercise," I replied. "It's obvious to us you're going to fight Russia."

"But that's ridiculous. We've a pact of non-aggression with them."

"You may think so, but I'm quite sure in my own mind that very soon you'll be at war with Russia."

Both the Paymaster and Prince Hohenlohe, who had heard, laughed at my stupidity.

The same day the German office clerk visited us. Since he was a fervent Nazi we tackled him about the unusual Army movements. But he gave us no new information, and repeated that Germany and Russia were to have combined exercises to prepare for the final attack on England. After that "Churchill and all other criminals would be made prisoner, tried and executed in a manner fitting their wickedness".

Crete fell: could nothing stem the German war machine?

On the morning of 22nd June I was woken by stones being thrown at the window. It was not yet 6 a.m., and almost two hours before the Sunday work parties left. Stones continued rattling on the window pane; I got up and opened the window. My friendly guard, to whom I gave English lessons, was standing outside very excited.

"Haven't you heard the news? Russia is in the war! It's the greatest thing that has happened. They will soon be side by side with your own men. *Deutschland ist Kaputt.*" With that he did a little dance then went on his rounds. We rarely came across a self-confessed German Communist and what he told me hardly seemed possible, even though we had seen for ourselves this vast movement of traffic eastward. I woke the others. As the full impact of the news dawned on us, we found ourselves visualizing a quick return home. Fred Neeve dressed and went to listen into the early morning B.B.C. news. Back he came and confirmed everything.

When the German clerk came to check working parties, it was obvious from his look that he had had bad news. We could not resist taunting him in his misery.

"What is wrong with you this morning; don't you feel well, Adam?"

"We have had some terrible news," he said.

"What do you mean—is Adolf Hitler dead?"

He jumped to attention and saluted on hearing our shocking insult to his Führer. "The Russian swine have attacked and tried to stab us in the back."

"If it is true that they've attacked you, how do you account for all that military stuff which has been going east for nearly two months now?"

"That is just a coincidence. They've betrayed us and my beloved Führer is going to teach them a lesson. Within six months from now Russia will be finished, and England will beg terms from us."

The first feeling of elation began to leave us as news came in of huge German advances and successes. They claimed that in the first few days of the new war over 4,000 planes had been destroyed and hundreds of thousands of P.O.W.s taken. We applied to the Prince to have air-raid shelters built in the camp, wanting to be prepared in case the Russians attempted to bomb the works, and hit us by mistake. He laughed and said, "There won't be any Russian bombing round here. At the present pace, the war will be over before you got any shelters finished."

Two weeks later Russian prisoners began to arrive; we'd never seen such a dirty-looking mob. They were all starving; their food supply could barely keep them alive.

It was a repetition of us a year earlier, only worse.

# 5

## *The Busy Life of Prisoners—1941*

With Russia in the war most men took a new lease of life, especially when we heard that Churchill would accept them as Allies, even though he would not withdraw any word he'd ever said against Communism. Mail and Red Cross parcels were now more regular.

But some had sad news from home—relatives killed in air raids—homes destroyed—even broken marriages. It was a case of going off the rails—"She had a drink too many that night" and someone else's baby was on the way. We wondered how many others lapsed like that without such obvious evidence. It was peculiar the way some P.O.W.s reacted to such news, especially those with girlfriends out on the Baustelle. One came storming into Room 3, and showed us a letter with the old story in it.

"I want you to obtain the necessary papers so that I can get a divorce."

"Have you thought the thing out carefully?"

"Of course I have. There is no other answer; I want a divorce!"

"But don't you realize that what your wife has done is no worse than what you are doing each day with your Polish girlfriend?"

"That's entirely different. I'm a man; I need it, and can do as I please! She's a woman and the consequences are so much worse if she does anything. She must keep straight."

"Don't you think you could take the view that what you're doing is enough to cancel out the one error of your wife?"

"No, I don't; and in any case I don't believe the story about the drink and the one night out. How d'you account for the fact that I've been married to her for four years and we still have no kids?"

"You should know the answer to that. How long have you had your Polish girl?"

"There's no need for your bloody rudeness. That won't make me change my mind!" He went away and we put in motion—through the Red Cross—the machinery for his divorce.

Quite different in attitude was a man who was a regular attender at the church services, and one who had absolutely nothing to do with females outside the camp. So far as the Germans were concerned he was a model prisoner, causing no trouble and doing any work he was given. When he received his bitter letter he asked me to help him write to his wife telling her he understood, and that he wanted arrangements made to adopt the child.

I began to wonder what would happen if I received a like letter; the true helplessness of P.O.W. life would then be brought right home and each day would become a hell on earth. When one of the seven in our room received such a tragic letter, our hearts went out to him.

The Germans were now becoming worried about the well-fed English fraternizing with women, during the day out on the Baustelle. The men went out to work at 6 a.m. and so did the women. The German bosses came an hour later. There was free time at lunch and the men roamed round the Baustelle with the greatest of ease, even swimming in the canal, especially in the summer of 1943. On other working parties, when they were replacing the men working in the fields, there were ample opportunities for fraternization. Even German girls were falling for the lures contained in Red Cross food parcels. If they were caught with a P.O.W., their hair was shorn and they were ridiculed by their compatriots. When one of our men, Jim White, was caught in the act with his Fräulein (a German witness had seen them go into a wash-house and shut the door, and had then described what he had seen through the keyhole), White was tried before a civil court and given a five-year sentence in the civil jail; the girl, who was just eighteen, was sentenced to two years. But that night, before he left the E/3 cells we managed to spirit him out, and he returned to E/3 to live underground as an extra while the Germans went searching for him all over the countryside.

The Germans next published their edict: "Sexual intercourse between P.O.W.s and any females is *verboten*. Intercourse with a German girl is punishable by death."

The sliding scale of penalties ranged from ten years for relations with a Dutch girl and five years for French, to one with a Pole and seven days with a Ukrainian. The men knew the ratings: few now went for Fräuleins.

Some P.O.W.s were building the Baustelle offices, and when finished, our painters moved in to decorate them. A gang of arrogant Fräuleins arrived, well trained in the Bund Deutscher Mädel—the League of German Girls. They came to boss the Polish girls who were forced to work in the canteens or labour on the job. One Fräulein commanded an E/3 signwriter to print in English a sign over their door. In big letters he painted BROTHEL—and told the Fräuleins it meant "House of Beauty"—a word without German equivalent. Their faces glowed with satisfied smiles, but smartly changed when officials from Berlin inspected progress. One understood English, and when he saw the word above the office door he stormed. There were red faces when he pointed out that the word Brothel was the same as the German *Bude*. But by then we had transferred the signwriter to another part of the Baustelle. They never traced him.

The same official, still touring, was accompanied by high-ranking Italian officers. As they rounded the gasometer one of our painters working on top accidentally dropped—or so it seemed—a large paint pot. It fell over the Italian who now had red stripes from top to toe. The luckless painter was hauled before the Germans; but, since it seemed to be only an accident, they just admonished him.

Although the officials had ostensibly come to see progress on the Baustelle, they had other reasons. For some time now the Germans had been concerned because the food they were delivering to the cookhouses on the Baustelle did not feed all their civilian 'slave' workers. They were puzzled because they were sure that nobody was getting more than his ladleful of soup, and only then on production of the official ticket. A civilian worker could draw his ration at any one of several cookhouses, providing he had the correct ticket, and each day the colour was changed, and all old tickets destroyed. The Germans considered their system foolproof. What they did *not* know was that we had discovered where the used tickets were placed ready to be destroyed, and that we had started up a roaring trade selling them for Reichmarks to the civilian workers—Poles, Czechs, Jugoslavs, Dutch and French.

For a whole month we had kept a watchful eye on the tickets issued by the Germans and had been able to figure out how the colour code worked. It seemed easy to sell the coloured tickets according to the day; what we needed was a man willing to take the risk—were he caught he could be shot—and one whom we could trust to keep his mouth shut.

At that time I had a strange encounter in my canteen. One man had stayed behind and waited until I had finished serving, then said, "Evening, Quarter, is it true that you come from Sunbury-on-Thames?"

"Yes, I do, but why do you ask?"

"Well, I come from Ashford Common."

"But that's next door to Sunbury."

"Of course it is, in fact most of my work is in Sunbury, and I often used to see you there in your red car."

"Then why the devil haven't you made yourself known to me before?"

"Simply because I didn't want any favours from you. But now that I receive Red Cross parcels and can get all I want on the job, I don't mind."

"Well, that's a damned silly reason, but I'm glad you've turned up at last—what's your name?"

"Jimmy Newcomb. I live opposite the old Spellhome Inn."

The more I got to know Jimmy, the better I liked him. He was dark and thick-set with a steely determined eye. More, he was unflappable and showed a great sense of humour. He was a man I could trust implicitly. He seemed the man for the food racket. He feared nobody and his mouth was shut tighter than an oyster.

Since he worked near where the tickets were destroyed, he could easily pinch them. He agreed. We decided to tell a few trusted civilians that tickets would be for sale the following week. The civilians would know when Jimmy was operating because that day he would wear a vivid red tie. No red tie—no operation! He would go to one of the *Aborts* (deep-pit latrines) on the Baustelle and sit in style while the civilians came to buy for Reichmarks another ladleful of "soup-de-jour". This swelled our hoard of much needed

Reichmarks, for we were paid for our work in camp in Lagermarks, which were totally useless outside E/3. (On average it was a princely 4 marks 30 pfennigs each week, which was equivalent to 10 shillings, for eleven hours' work per day, plus seven hours on Saturday and often a half-day on Sunday).

As word spread around the Baustelle about the ticket sales, queues waiting for Jimmy grew longer and he found he needed to co-opt Phil Kirby to keep the line in order. Whenever the Germans appeared on the scene, Jimmy reluctantly, yet quickly, disposed of his unsold tickets down the hole, where not even Gestapo sleuths would search.

The system went well for several months and, though Newcomb and Kirby had some close shaves, they escaped detection. With continued food losses, the Germans were out for blood, and several German canteen officials, accused of inefficiency, quietly disappeared. Then they started a new ticket system we could not break into, and thus we lost a good source of Reichmarks.

Later Newcomb, Kirby and I were out on the job seeking what was useful or valuable, when we walked into one of the large canteens, decorated with the Nazi colours of red and black. The walls were covered with photographs of Hitler, Himmler, Heydrich, Goebbels, Goering and the rest of the gang. In a corner was a dixie of mashed potato. Three minds had one single thought: the photographs were soon plastered. We were surveying our master mess when eight German girls walked in, appalled that their beloved Führer had become a coconut shy! We bolted.

We learnt later that the Fräuleins—though they had described us—were themselves strafed in a correction camp near Berlin.

Then the Gestapo started looking for the English criminals. To remove Newcomb from that hot spot I told Prince Hohenlohe that I needed help in the canteen and library: Newcomb who lived near me at home could be trusted. Surprisingly, the Prince agreed and Newcomb joined camp staff. Since he would ask no questions nor talk, I was able to devote much more time to my secret work which was mounting now that the Russians were in the war.

There was enough space in the canteen for Newcomb's

bed, which suited me for I could work late there on the excuse that I was talking camp finance and camp prices with him. As it was next to the German guard room—with the barbed-wire fence between—no one suspected that the canteen had become the centre for illicit operations and espionage. Meanwhile, had the Germans troubled to look under his bed, they would have found a radio, camera, civilian clothing and Reichmarks, all on the *strengstens verboten* list.

It was August, and the weather right for escapes. These needed most careful planning, maps, method, food and compasses. We found maps in Kapitza's store in Ehrenforst and compasses were arriving in parcels from England. The Germans regularly raided and searched the rooms.

Just before one such raid, Newcomb, anxious about my Zeiss camera, slipped it into his pocket, walked nonchalantly past the guard at the gate and round the corner towards Prince Hohenlohe's office. Outside was a garden tended by one of our camp staff.

"Morning, Jim, what the dickens are you doing out here so early?" he asked suspiciously.

"Morning, Bill, just getting a spot of fresh air."

He walked up to the window box outside the Prince's window, lifted out a plant pot of blue lobelia, put the camera in the box, then replaced the plant on top.

"Hey Jim, what d'you think you're doing there?"

"Just hiding something. There's a big search on today."

"But you can't do that—if they find it they'll say I put it there, and I'll get shot."

"You're wrong. First, *I* put it there—not you—and it's going to stay there. Second, if they shoot you there won't be anything more for you to worry about, will there?"

With that he walked back into the canteen and waited for the search, which as usual found nothing important.

Next morning Prince Hohenlohe on his camp rounds looked into the canteen. "How do you feel this lovely summer's morning, Newcomb?" he asked.

"As fit as a fiddle with all strings busted!"

"I beg your pardon, I do not quite understand that phrase," replied the Prince. In explaining the expression Newcomb gained the friendship of the Prince, and our canteen became even more inviolate.

Our next move was to contact other camps around the Baustelle so that articles could be exchanged to our mutual benefit. Paymaster Brauner, who took a percentage of all our sales for himself, helped keep our stocks up. The Prince agreed that representatives of other camps could come to buy canteen goods in E/3, and so another link was forged in our escape chain.

To Ehrenforst at that time came a working party of Palestinian Jews who had been in the British Army caught in Greece in 1941. As "British" they were treated like us; not like *die Juden* from Germany and Poland. Several indeed had actually left Upper Silesia when the Nazis gained power in 1932. Their senior N.C.O. came to see me. We learned that these Jews could obtain as much German money as we needed, for they knew many Germans in the area. And what was more they were prepared to trade with us on the basis of one ordinary Reichmark for one Lagermark—a much better exchange rate than we were able to get so far.

The Jews not only became very good canteen customers, but through them we accumulated larger supplies of money for exchange purposes and could get German travel papers (*Ausweis*) for escapers.

We knew that the chance of getting home after escaping from Upper Silesia was slim, but none the less the chance had to be taken. With almost the whole of Europe under the Nazis, there appeared to be little chance of hiding up, but gradually through contacts with civilian workers and with other camps, we were able to learn of "helpers" in France and Belgium. With what I then knew I often felt like making a break myself; but realized I had to stay behind: there was so much more important work to do. Also I had a growing aim to get to Berlin as soon as possible for I now felt that all other work in E/3 could be safely left in the hands of Newcomb.

Two escapers left disguised as husband and wife. Though it seemed long odds, we fitted them out for their long journey. Having changed into civilian clothes on the Baustelle they started off in brilliant sunshine.

They had gone about a mile through the forest when they sensed they were being followed. "Let's get down on the grass as if we were wooing," *Kraft durch Freude* (strength through joy). Two Germans following them walked past looking the other way, not wishing to stop a possible increase in the Führer's population. Ten miles further on, when passing through a village that lay between them and their first "link", a door suddenly opened just ahead. Out poured a stream of Brownshirts.

"Blimey, what happens next?"

"Just keep on walking as if nothing was wrong." But an efficient Brownshirt stopped them and asked for their identity cards. They both produced their British Army paybooks. The German looked at the books, shook his head and frowned. Puzzled he said,

"What are these?"

"They're our identity cards—we are *Ausländer* [foreigners]."

When the Brownshirt started asking awkward questions, they owned up.

"We're English escaped prisoners."

"But that's nonsense—there're no English women prisoners in this area."

"But we're both *men*, escaped from Blechhammer."

"Don't tell lies. What about your Frau with her lovely figure?"

So the "lady" removed her "lovely figure" and handed the Brownshirt two pads of cotton wool. It was a bedraggled pair that were duly delivered back to E/3 and locked in the cells for a week.

Many had found they could barter with German civilians using cigarettes and chocolate from their personal parcels that now came regularly. The guards checked each man at the gate each night. Some had the brilliant idea of putting eggs into muslin and carrying them in under their hats. This worked well until someone bragged to the guards. Then one night, the usual search of haversacks and packets over, the guards suddenly went along the lines flipping off the P.O.W.s' hats with their fists. Yellowy slime trickled slowly down their cheeks. But not to be outdone, they next broke the eggs into condoms, then slipped the condoms on. The guards, carefully body-searching, coarsely remarked how much better endowed the prisoners were than themselves, and with reluctant respect let them go. Likewise with potatoes in short supply, they simply threaded wire through two, then placed the V of the wire on the fork of their pants. The guards again learnt to respect the size of British genitalia.

Civilian clothing came in worn under uniforms, for we were never strip-searched.

By now we had a number of guards in our pay, and if something was urgently wanted which we could not smuggle into the camp, we simply arranged for one of them to bring it in. He would bring the parcel into the camp on the pretext of having his uniform altered by our camp "tailor", or he would come in with our stuff when he showered—for the German bath-house was still on our side of the wire. But in total war, even guards were liable to be searched before entering camp.

With the canteen above suspicion most Germans felt I was working on their side, and luckily most P.O.W.s were suspicious of my friendship with the enemy. Every day in Room 3 came arguments with the others. I was bluntly told to stop playing up to the bloody Germans. Many times I wanted to ask them to use their own intelligence and try to imagine what type of work I was doing; but I was always struck by the thought that perhaps one of them would unwittingly betray me. Further, I had been sworn to secrecy; and so, I had to grin and bear the fierce banter that showed they felt I really was keep on our captors. It was not pleasant risking my life for my country, yet being called a collaborator by my own countrymen.

After quarrels such as these I found a great relief in going to the canteen and either doing my work for England in silence or chatting about things from home with Jim Newcomb. He was always so understanding and helpful, and he seemed to sense when I had special work to do, for he would make himself scarce and leave me alone with my thoughts.

I was spending long hours with Prince Hohenlohe, trying to find out some way to get to Berlin. The Prince was not keen to discuss German politics. But he suggested that I should write an article for the P.O.W. weekly *The Camp*, which was distributed all over Germany. This he said might help me to Berlin, especially if I mentioned that P.O.W. life to date has not been too bad. I wrote an article entitled "A Year Passes",* in which I reviewed what had happened

* See Appendix, p. 149.

since being captured and I made it as provocative as possible, hoping it would catch the eye of somebody of importance. Yet I knew such an article in that paper would make me even more suspect to my fellow prisoners. All the time it was a game of creating the right atmosphere. The article was published in September 1941, but no invitation to visit Berlin came through. I knew that the Prince was deceived by it, while the camp inmates became even more convinced than ever that I was up to no good.

By now, with a fair supply of sports equipment, we began international soccer matches. I was lucky enough—or perhaps big enough—to be selected to "goal" for England, and could hold my place. I had fortunately played in goal for my school and an Old Boys team, and found the exercise good. The Germans could not understand how English P.O.W.s had such energy when playing soccer and so little when on the Baustelle working for them.

By December, most rooms were making preparations for Christmas, which was to be very different from the abysmal one of 1940. By gentle coaching the art of brewing had been taught fairly successfully and some potent mixtures were bottled ready for the festivities. Despite the Heath Robinson distilling plants, the results were drinkable.

Jack Hobbs in Room 3 was busy writing music for the bands and we were all looking forward to the 25th of December. Many felt confident this would be their last in captivity; but the war news showed we would likely spend several more Christmases in Germany with Hitler.

Christmas Day dawned bitterly cold; but 300 men turned up for church service. On Christmas Eve the Germans had wept at the strains of their lovely "Silent Night, Holy Night". What a horrible farce it all was, and what hypocrites men are, both sides worshipping the Prince of Peace, yet willing to kill each other burning with hatred in their hearts.

The bands gave us a concert in the afternoon: military, dance and Hawaiian music, followed by a show, "Mary's Black Eye". Even the Germans had tried to give us better fare, but their offering was scorned. For besides the weekly parcel and fifty cigarettes, that year we each had an extra "Christmas parcel", containing special items—Christmas pudding, cake and chocolate biscuits. It was indeed a feast.

I had almost forgotten about my article in *The Camp*, and had given up all hope of ever reaching Berlin, when one morning in January 1942, Adam, the German Schreiber, summoned me to the Prince who said, "You are to pack all your kit at once and be prepared to move off this afternoon. You're wanted in Lamsdorf." I did not like his use of the word "wanted".

"Have you any idea why I have to go?"

"I'm not supposed to tell you, but I believe you're being taken to Berlin for questioning." That sounded more ominous and I was very worried that my secret work had been discovered; if so, I wondered just how much had been found out.

"Can you tell me any more about the message you have received?" I asked.

"There is nothing more to tell you; but I would advise you to be extremely careful in what you say, and please leave *me* out of the picture in case they get the idea that I'm being too lenient with British prisoners."

Deep in thought I left the Prince. The moment I entered Room 3 I broke the news. From the looks they gave me it was obvious their worst thoughts about me were now confirmed.

"What are you going to do when you get there?"

"I know as much about that as you do."

"But you must have some idea."

"I tell you I haven't the foggiest notion."

"Well, it's quite clear to us you've been playing up to the Prince for some time, and no doubt he thinks you can help the bloody Nazis."

"Of course I've been playing up to the Prince, but hasn't the camp benefited by my attitude?"

That was a sore point with the others; but it was something that could not be easily denied.

Then Moggy butted in, "I suppose I'll have to run the canteen for you while you're away."

"There's no need for you to do anything of the sort. I've already arranged with the Prince for Jim Newcomb to carry on in my absence."

"But he's only a bloody gunner."

"Maybe, but he's got his head screwed on right, and I'm quite sure he'll manage better than anyone else." No matter how I tried I could not convince them that in choosing Newcomb, I was striving for the good of the camp.

That afternoon I left Blechhammer, not with good wishes from the others, but entirely alone—under a depressing cloud of suspicion that I had become a Nazi.

# 6

## *William Joyce, Gentleman—Traitor*

I arrived back at Lamsdorf on 31st January 1942, and found that my doubtful reputation had preceded me. I was closely questioned by the British Camp Security who thus foolishly exposed themselves, for had I been really working for the Germans I could have "shopped" them all.

Luckily I found some good friends in the Reception Barrack. The barrack interpreter, Cecil Sklan, did all he could to make me comfortable and I sensed he somehow knew about my work. I also found another member of my unit there, Fred Blewitt, who for some reason had fallen foul of Lamsdorf Camp Security. When they saw the two of us were friendly, suspicion increased towards us, especially as I had daily contact with the German Sonderführer Meyer.

I was most anxious to leave Lamsdorf and find out what awaited me in Berlin. Eventually I was told I would leave for Berlin on Monday 9th March—with two armed guards for company. It seemed I was now an important prisoner; but whether for my own good or ill remained to be seen.

Most of the trains were moving troops to and from the Russian Front and as we waited at Breslau station it looked as if we would never get on one. So I suggested to my guards that they should tell the stationmaster I was a very important prisoner, as could be seen from my red and blue artillery hat which had always impressed the Germans. The trick worked and we were soon led to a carriage of high-ranking German officers. One of them, a colonel, started whispering to my guards, then turned to me and said, "*Herr General, sprechen Sie Deutsch?*" I told him I understood only a little German and in broken English he asked me how many other generals had been captured. I did not disillusion him and a desultory conversation continued until we all fell fast asleep. I wondered what would befall me on the morrow. Doubtless the German officers in the carriage were thinking how unusual it would be to tell their wives and women that they had talked to a British general on his way to Berlin for "special purposes".

We reached Berlin in the early hours of the morning and from the Lehnter Bahnhof had a fair walk to our destination. There was little outward sign of any bombing, though one bridge had been destroyed. The guards laughed when I pointed this out, telling me that Berlin—unlike London— was immune to air attack. Goering had guaranteed that.

It was 9 o'clock when we arrived at Stalag IIID— Steglitz—in the north-west. To my surprise it was just a large block of offices which had formerly been a gown warehouse; but the owner—a Jew—was now in a concentration camp. The Stalag seemed a hive of industry, and I saw a large stock of Red Cross parcels and a stock of British uniforms. I was introduced to a Major Heimpel who said he was in charge of counter-espionage in P.O.W. camps. This was hardly reassuring, but his smooth manner allayed my doubts.

"You must be very tired and dirty after your most uncomfortable train journey."

"I would certainly feel much better with a wash."

"Sure—right away, and when you're ready I'll have a meal for you."

I sat down to a decent meal prepared from Red Cross parcels. Major Heimpel, reading my mind, said, "Don't think you're robbing anybody else of that food. The International Red Cross allows a few parcels here to feed anyone passing through Berlin." I wondered how much of that food reached the hungry mouths of genuine British prisoners, and how much went to the Englishmen such as William Joyce—Lord Haw-Haw—who were busy denouncing their country in broadcasts and propaganda pamphlets.

"You're going to a very nice Kommando in Berlin," continued Major Heimpel, "and after you've been interviewed you'll be allowed to go for walks in the city, accompanied of course by a guard."

"Are there any other Englishmen there?"

"You will share a room with an Australian who has been there for some time."

"I don't understand why I've been brought to Berlin."

"You'll find out much more about that after you've been interviewed. You have nothing to worry about, have you?"

I assured him hastily that I was puzzled more than anything. Indeed the walks seemed a heaven-sent opportunity for me to use my eyes in the city; and I could not for the life of me see why the head of German counter-intelligence should provide it for me. All I could gather was that my new home sounded like the place where doubtful prisoners passed through before the Germans gave them special tasks. I would have to tread warily indeed and pit my wits against the man who, by his position, had to be the bitter enemy of a British spy.

After a short walk from the Stalag we reached a house in a residential part of Berlin, one of a row overlooking the River Spree. I noticed that my new address was 7 Schliefenaferstrasse and that there was no wire around the building. The front door was unguarded, and I was taken to the Feldwebel in charge of the Kommando. He was a villainous-looking man, with several fingers missing from his right hand.

"I understand from Major Heimpel that you are to be made as comfortable as possible, but until a visitor has been here you must remain within the house. You will find Frenchmen, Russians, Poles and various other nationalities here. You are not now allowed to speak to them, though if you want one of the Russians to clean your room for you that will be all right. But do not overpay any of them for what they do."

I thanked him for the tip and asked what the position was about meals.

"There is a cookhouse upstairs, run by the French, and you will also receive your Red Cross parcel and fifty cigarettes each week."

"And where do I wash clothes?"

"Don't worry about that—let the Ruskies do it for you, but be sure to count your articles when they are returned. Now let me take you along to meet your companion."

I met Lieutenant Ralph Holroyd from Sydney, Australia, who had received a nasty ankle wound in action in North Greece. He said he had early fallen foul of the Germans because of an escape, and had done ten days "solitary" in a cell in Lazarett-Lamsdorf. He had been summoned to Berlin for quite a different reason.

"You see, my mother is German, and she happened to be holidaying in Germany when the war broke out. As a German national she's not interned; but when I became captured and they found out that she was living in Essen, they said it could be possible for me to see her regularly—if I did what they wanted. I was chatted up by Sonderführers Meyer and Lange in Lamsdorf. You can be sure there will be a price and that will be to the detriment of my own country, or Allied cause."

"What are you going to do about it?" I asked him.

"Get all I can out of them first, and then tell them they can go to hell so far as I'm concerned. I'm quite sure my mother would want me to remain loyal to my country; and I'm afraid they may harm her when they realize I won't co-operate. But that's enough about me: tell me about yourself."

After I had told my story, we both realized we had to take everything concerning the other on trust, for either of us could be spying on the other for the Germans. But we both decided that the other's story was true, and from that moment a strong friendship grew up between us. The more I got to know him, the more I realized that Ralph was as fine and loyal a man as I had met in P.O.W. life.

The next few days were spent trying to find out a little about the other occupants of the house. At times the confusion of languages was really comical. If we spoke French to the Frenchmen they usually replied in German, while one of the Poles always spoke in French and the lone Belgian there usually spoke Dutch. One of the Russians at least spoke perfect English, and he acted as interpreter for his compatriots. His name was Mosalov and he said he had been head of the shipping section of Arcos House in London when the establishment was raided before the war. When Russia had come into the war he had held an important position in the Russian Government: it was his job to provide electricity for the factories which were being established well behind the lines, away from the German bombing. But because he had told his superiors that he would not be able to complete his task within the given time, he had been forced to divorce his wife and had been sent up to the front line where he had been captured. Mosalov was a man of very mixed moods and feelings; he had no time whatsoever for Stalin or Communism, and because of this the

Germans had tried to get him to work for them. But he hated them because of the way they had treated him on the march into Germany, and also for the way the Russian Kommissars were being shot out of hand if captured.

I thought perhaps after this Mosalov would have at least a friendly feeling for the British. But it was not so, for he could not forget the way we had raided Arcos House, and the so-called lies we had told about the propaganda machine working there. Deep down, too, he had engrained in him the Russian hatred of anything that could be classed as capitalistic. And so it was with almost all the Russians I met in this house of scheming. None of them had any time for Communism, but they had even less for England or Germany. And yet day after day they went out to work for the Germans, and when they came back at night they always seemed remarkably clean, as if they had been writing, perhaps broadcasting.

As far as the French were concerned I gathered that the British had had the temerity to fire on the French fleet at Dakar in Africa and even capture some of the fleet, thereby placing them out of reach of the Germans. But as the French argued that the British were in the wrong, they seemed to be potential converts to the Nazi creed. The Frenchmen played up to them for just as long as it took to organize an escape, and then they were off, much to the consternation of the Germans who thought them thoroughly unsporting.

The Belgian there was an interesting character. His name was Richere, and he claimed friendship with the king of the Belgians. He warned me to be very careful what I said and did in the house, as it was the headquarters for people of all nations who were friendly to the Nazis. He told me his job was to design the flowerbeds which ran down the sides of the autobahns, which seemed harmless enough. But I had the feeling that Richere was helping to organize the escape of the Frenchmen, and that he was liable to be more of a hindrance than a help to the German cause, although when talking to the Feldwebel or the guards he was always very friendly. I knew this meant nothing, and conversely that the man who had most to say against the Germans was quite often the one working for them. Some of the Sonderführers and guards were for ever defiling Hitler and the Nazi Party; but I had always known that a man was not allowed to hold the rank of Sonderführer unless he had some connection with the Party, and there was no doubt the Nazis obtained a lot of information by pretending to be critical.

Our room batman was a young Russian who came from Baku and hated the Germans vehemently because his family had been killed in the bombing. It was Mosalov who told us this, for the lad understood no German or English, so we could talk freely when he was in the room. But I could not help noticing that when he left our room our batman always seemed to make a beeline for the Feldwebel's office. So one day I followed him downstairs and as I passed the office I saw the lad inside talking away in fluent German. I heard enough to realize he was repeating word for word what Ralph Holroyd and I had just been saying in English. Not bad for someone who was not supposed to understand either language. Fortunately Ralph and I had been cautious, and I did not think the Feldwebel would be able to glean much from what he was told. All the same, our conversation became even more guarded, lest the Germans had bugged the building.

One morning the Feldwebel sent for me and said we were to prepare for two important visitors that afternoon. I gave Holroyd the message.

"Who d'you think is coming, John?"

"Somebody from the German security side to take a good look at us, I expect."

"Supposing one of the famous broadcasting people comes along—Lord Haw-Haw or Baillie-Stewart—would you recognize them?" Ralph asked.

"There'd be no mistaking Haw-Haw, or rather William Joyce to give him his real name. He was a prominent member of the British Union of Fascists, and he's got a big scar on his face which he collected while addressing a Fascist meeting somewhere in England."

"How d'you know so much about him?"

"I used to meet him sometimes when I visited the Fascist H.Q. Club in Chelsea with an officer friend of mine."

"It would be rather nasty if he remembers you from those days, wouldn't it?"

I did not like to tell Ralph it would be a good thing if it meant that I would gain the confidence of the Germans. There was so much secret work for me in Berlin; but first I had to gain some degree of freedom, and of that there was at present no sign.

On the dot of three o'clock the Feldwebel came in and told us to stand to attention for our visitors. Of the two men in civilian clothing who walked in, one was William Joyce, complete with cigar, and looking just as cocky as his broadcasts suggested. He looked hard at me but did not appear to know me.

"I should like to see these two gentlemen one at a time," he said in German to the Feldwebel. "Mr Brown, would you mind waiting outside?"

I turned to Ralph and said, "Ralph, please tell me what the German gentleman is saying, because as you know I don't understand German." Ralph translated fluently and apologized for my apparent lack of knowledge of German.

"Unfortunately I must speak in German," Joyce responded, "as I do not know any English; but my friend here will act as interpreter for us."

"I will go outside now," I said. "Gentlemen, as the room is so hot, would you like me to take your coats and hats and hang them on the pegs outside?"

They gave them to me and I went into an adjoining room. As soon as I was quite sure the coast was clear, I examined them thoroughly. I found that Joyce's hat was from Bond Street, and his overcoat from a shop in Regent Street, and in both hat and coat the initials WJ were plain to see. In the coat pockets I found a quantity of chocolates and English cigarettes (doubtless stolen from Red Cross supplies), and then in the inner pocket a letter written in English, and signed by Heimpel. It ran something like this:

Dear Mr Joyce,
It is the wish of Dr Goebbels that you should go to 7 Schliefenaferstrasse where you will find two prisoners, one English and the other Australian. The latter has a German mother, and we feel that with a little pressure through her, the son will be only too pleased to work for the Führer. The Englishman we would like to find out more about before proceeding in the matter. From reports we have received he is unpopular with his fellow prisoners because he speaks well of our nation, and we have had reports from other prisoners favourable to us that the

man Brown is a member of the British Fascist Party.
Because of this you may recognize him; but should you
do so, do not betray the fact to him. If you are able to find
out anything it is possible that this man will be most
useful to us in Berlin. Will you please report to me at ten
o'clock tomorrow morning, as Dr Goebbels is waiting for
our conclusions regarding the two men.

Heil Hitler!

So this was what we were up against. But before I had
time to decide what my line of action would be Ralph
Holroyd came into the room to say it was my turn.

"How did you get on?" I whispered as I passed him.

"Bloody awful. We had a quarrel. The rotten swine
wanted me to turn traitor on the promise of seeing my
mother. I would rather die first. Good luck to you, John."

"Ah come in, Mr Brown, and take a seat over here."

*"Bitte?"*

"Oh, of course you do not understand German. My friend
will have to help all the time."

I was very relieved for I knew I would be able to concentrate much better if I did not have to think in German.

"How long have you been a prisoner?"

"Two years."

"You must be longing to get outside to a civilized life,
and of course it would be nice to see a woman again,
wouldn't it?"

"That seems an unnecessary question when there is no
chance of it happening for some years to come."

"You must not be too sure about *that*. We Germans have
our ways and means, you know. Tell me, do you ever listen
to the radio nowadays?"

"It is forbidden for us to listen to England, but in
Blechhammer we used to hear Lord Haw-Haw each day."

Joyce pricked up his ears when I mentioned his broadcasting name.

"And what do you think of him?"

"Well, I used to listen to him quite a lot before the war."

"Why did you?"

"We used to get a lot of fun out of him in those days."

He gave me a black look but went on, "What did you
listen on, the short or the medium wave?"

"On both, but the short wave came through better." I said this because I had never heard him on anything but the medium-wave band.

"Would you know Lord Haw-Haw if you saw him?"

"No, I'm afraid not, I do not even know who he is."

"Have you seen me anywhere before?"

"No, I have not."

"Well, maybe you did laugh at Lord Haw-Haw's broadcasts before the war, but the people of England are not laughing now that the British Empire is finished, and the Japs will be in Singapore any day." I noted with glee that the more Joyce talked, the more atrocious his German became.

"That is news to me—I have not seen a paper or heard the German news for several days."

"I mentioned before that we could make it possible for you to go out and meet a girlfriend, but you must be prepared to do a little work for us first."

"You must understand that as a British prisoner-of-war, I am bound by the Geneva Convention."

Joyce seemed displeased with my reply, and the interview came to an end shortly afterwards. I felt that I had at least put him off the scent, for I had evaded most of his questions, and had probably not seemed very bright to him. But I was worried about Ralph, for it was obvious that Joyce would put in a stinking report about his attitude. Indeed within three days Ralph was given marching orders, told to pack his kit and be ready to move off the next morning for an "unknown destination". It sounded ominously like a punishment camp.

"Don't worry, John, wherever they send me they won't break my spirit. Besides, I've had a note from my mother saying I'm doing the right thing in refusing their filthy offer."

I did not ask Ralph how he had received such a message, but I was greatly relieved to be right in my judgement of his integrity.

"I'll try to find out from the Jerries where they're taking you, and if you receive the parcels which I'll ask the Red Cross to send, perhaps you could acknowledge them—then at least I'll know you're in a position to write."

"I'll do that, John, and before I go I'd like to say this. At first I thought you might be one of those Nazi narks, but now I'm quite sure you have a mission of some sort, and certainly *not* for the Germans."

"What do you mean by a mission, Ralph? You know of course I'm most interested in Y.M.C.A. work."

"You know jolly well I don't mean the Y.M.C.A., but don't worry. I'm not going to ask you questions which I know you mustn't answer. I don't want to hear you tell me lies as you do the Jerries."

That night we sat down to our final meal together, and we had representatives of all the other nations in with us, each assuring Ralph not to worry about me as they would look after me.

When the Feldwebel came in for roll call the next morning he told Ralph to report to his office, then turned to me and said, "I have some news for you too this morning. You must have pleased your questioners, for from now on you can go out walking in the town, as long as you have a guard with you."

"How often can I go?"

"As often as you like, providing there's a guard available."

"And where can I go in the town?"

"Anywhere you wish, but if you go in the shops you must report to me exactly what you buy."

"Could I have a map to see the various beauty spots of Berlin?"

"Certainly, I'll get Jan [one of the guards] to buy you a good one."

I thus started on my sight-seeing tours of Berlin. I decided to cover every part of it, so that no item of interest to home would be missed. The guards took a poor view of my walking ability; but if they had seen me with my feet in a bowl of hot water each night perhaps they would not have minded so much. Some seemed to enjoy themselves, particularly when high-ranking officers saluted my red artillery cap. This strange freedom was certainly enjoyable after the barbed wire of the other camps; but I knew all the time that one false step would be the end of my outings, and in all probability of me.

Within a few weeks I had information regarding airfields, hidden factories, camouflage, ack-ack defences, and much else which would be of use to the Allies when the bombing of Berlin started in earnest. And so my messages home increased dramatically. At first I feared they would be intercepted by the Germans, but in due course I received assurances from England that all was not in vain and information should indeed by stepped up.

I next received a letter from Nan which was most uncomplimentary to the Germans (she of course still knew nothing of my secret service work). It was unfortunate, as I had always persuaded them that my wife was as sympathetic to them as I was—had we not spent holidays together in Germany before the war? Hastily I sent a secret message asking that my wife be told not to say too much in her letters. Back in Sunbury-on-Thames Nan received a letter from the War Office asking her to call as soon as possible. With misgivings she reported to the address given, and was met by a young officer.

"Mrs Brown, what have you been saying in your letters to your husband?"

"Nothing out of the ordinary," she replied.

"Are you quite sure about that? We have had a message from Mr Brown asking you to be very careful about what you say in your letters. Your husband is engaged in some special work, and nothing you say must endanger him. You need not worry about his safety providing you say nothing to anybody about him, and do not disclose why you have come here this morning."

That was the end of the interview, but Nan became seriously worried when there were hardly any letters from me during the next three months. I later found out that all my post was being held up by Major Heimpel because he had suspicions.

During the days that followed in Berlin, there were occasional air-raid warnings, but no sign of damage, and it was safe enough to stay in bed during the alarms. Almost every day men were passing through the Kommando, and I picked up what information I could from them. During my walks through the town I was sickened by sights such as a whole family, from grandparents down to young children of three or four, all marked with the Jewish star on their backs, and scorned by the German population. My guard would tell me that this family was lucky; they were good Jews, and had been allowed to work for the Germans. I would say nothing, but one day, in a moment of compassion, I gave one family some chocolate and cigarettes. I was reported to the Feldwebel; my walks and parcels were stopped for a week, and I was warned very sternly to keep away from the civilian population.

The respite indoors gave me time to catch up with my writing and also an opportunity to nurse Mosalov, who had been taken seriously ill. I passed on what food I could spare from my Red Cross parcels; the Russians received no help from the Protecting Power as their Government was not a signatory to the Geneva Convention, and civilian parcels from Russia were forbidden by the Nazis and Stalin whose edict was, "Russian soldiers taken prisoner are traitors to Mother Russia and can expect death at the end of the war"! So the poor devils were between two fires: at home counted as dead, and in Germany condemned as Communists and fed worse than animals until such time as they were willing to give the Nazi salute and work against Russia.

As soon as Mosalov was well again, all the Russians were removed from the house. The day they went I was at the Stalag collecting letters, and when I returned I found a note from Mosalov.

You have regarded me as a friend during the last four weeks, but you ought to know that I hate the English as much if not more than the Germans, who are willing to give me a home after they have won the war and beaten your country so badly that she will never again dictate to the world. You think you have been kind to me while I have been ill, by giving me a few cigarettes, but had you been a true comrade to the Russians you would have given your Red Cross parcels to us each week. Perhaps when Germany has won the war, and I am on their side I will be able to repay you in a like manner.

To say I'd been slapped in the face was to put it mildly, and at once my mind started racing over the last few weeks to see if I'd said or done anything at all to give the game away. But time alone would show if I had made a fatal error.

The house had been emptied to allow some Indian officers to be brought in, and within a day or two the reason for their presence became obvious. One evening a meeting was called and I was requested to attend. Joyce was there and he opened the meeting by running over all the evil England had done, and how she had robbed India. Then a high-ranking officer made an impassioned appeal to the Indians to join the Germans, saying that Hitler would give full support to an Indian regiment and would guarantee complete independence once England had been subdued. His whole speech was inflammatory and nationalistic and I thought that anything could happen. But as soon as he had finished an Indian stepped forward.

"As Senior Officer here, I speak for my fellow officers. We regard *you* as a traitor not only to England but to our own dear land. We will have nothing to do with your foul schemes. England has promised us that as soon as the war is over we shall be free. We have no reason to doubt her word. I give you five minutes in which to leave this room. After that I will not be responsible for my fellow officers."

His speech was wildly acclaimed and on an impulse I rushed forward and shook the Indian officer by the hand. A bad mistake I realized as soon as I turned and saw Joyce eyeing me with hatred. He had registered a serious black mark against me.

The walks resumed but I feared they would soon be curtailed. I was accordingly anxious to find out about Templehof Aerodrome and persuaded the guard to go that way. He said that for security reasons I could not go too near. While we were walking along the road and past a public lavatory I said I wanted to use it. As I expected he waited outside and I went straight through the building, out the other side, and walked away as fast as I could. Having made my survey of the area and found much of interest, I decided it was high time to get back to the house. But my luck was out. I was stopped by a policeman who was not a bit satisfied with my explanation that I had lost my guard and was going straight back to camp. They took me to the police station and I was about to be questioned when the air-raid alarm went and guns could be heard firing. At once all went to the cells downstairs. Soon the policemen were playing the favourite card game called Skat at which I considered myself fairly skilful. When one player had to go upstairs to answer the telephone, I asked if I could join in.

"You don't know how to play this German game."

"Yes I do, I've learnt to play it from our guards."

"Sit down then: but it's your own fault if you lose all your money."

And so we played, and luck was with me, so much so that within half an hour most men wanted to finish. Meanwhile, I'd produced English chocolate and cigarettes and had handed them round on the basis of "chocolate for the kiddy and a few fags for the wife and yourself". When the all-clear sounded, the station officer said to me, "We're going to let you go because you have been so kind to us; but please go straight back to your camp and say that you got separated from your guard during the raid. He is sure to say the same to protect his own skin."

When I got back to the house I duly told my story, and found that my guard had not yet returned. When he did he came up to see me, and said he had told exactly the same story. So all was well: or so we thought.

But three days later Heimpel told me I was going back to Lamsdorf. When I asked why he said I was making a nuisance of myself.

"I heard what you did at the meeting of Indian officers, and you are showing far too much interest in Templehof Aerodrome and other such places."

"Simply because I am very interested in Berlin and the district."

"That may be so, but I have decided to send you back to Lamsdorf."

I said I wanted to go back to my working party at Blechhammer and he said he would see to it, adding that he supposed I was anxious to see my old friend Prince Hohenlohe. There was a distinct sneer in his voice. I could tell he not only suspected me but was not too sure about the Prince either.

In Heimpel I had acquired a formidable enemy.

# 7

## *Cockney Nazi*

My reception at Lamsdorf was extremely mixed, nor was I popular when I gave the latest war news. I was glad to leave Lamsdorf with all its N.C.O. scroungers who could have done a much better job helping on the working parties.

It was a lovely day in August 1942 when I got back to Blechhammer and was greeted by Jim Newcomb. There had been much gossip while I was away. Rumours put around had aroused strong feeling against me; one even said I would never be allowed to set foot again inside the camp. Furthermore, the sergeant-majors had tried to get Newcomb out of the canteen, but Prince Hohenlohe had kept his word: he had stayed; Jack Hobbs had supervised.

Desmond Cribb had left in April, and was replaced by a New Zealand doctor, Captain John Borrie. There were several other New Zealanders, mostly taken in Crete. Many had it tough after capture. Two of them, Captains Noakes and Warren, were dentists and the others medical orderlies.

In my absence there had been much change. There was now a camp hall, a Medical Inspection Room (M.I. room), and a three-ward hospital, all beautifully painted, as were most of the camp rooms. Community spirit was much stronger.

I commented on all the changes to Newcomb and asked about the Baustelle.

"The best job of all now is the building going on just across the Adolf Hitler Canal. It's a brothel for foreign workers. *Les dames* have recently arrived from France, and our boys can't wait to get the place and the girls into proper working order."

I asked whether Jim White—who had been sentenced for having relations with a Fräulein—had been caught. He said, "No, he's still hiding in the camp, though he's had one or two narrow escapes during searches. When he feels he wants a woman he changes places with someone on one of the parties. But I think he's being foolhardy. One day they'll catch him."

"Has Ron Gray heard anything more from his wife since he adopted her baby last year?"

"Blimey, you really *are* out of date. She's had another kid since then—usual story—just once after drinks. He's believed her again, and has agreed to adopt the second!"

"Well, that's stretching it a bit far."

"What I thought too; but you've got to admire him!"

I went along to Room 3 prepared to do battle. Otto was making tea and nearly dropped the water when I walked in.

"What the hell are you doing here, Busty?"

"I've just come back from Berlin. Heard a rumour I would never be allowed inside this camp again!"

Otto looked very uncomfortable. "Don't be a bloody fool, Busty—but you must admit we had every right to wonder what was going on, mate!" Otto never minced his words.

"And when I've told my story, you'll still have every right because you can rest assured you won't get much from me."

I met John Borrie, Warren and Noakes. Then I told my story. They listened patiently, but it was obvious I was not believed by most.

"Well, Busty, you've told a pretty remarkable story, and you can't expect us to believe it unless you tell us why the Jerries sent you to Berlin in the first place."

"Don't you understand plain English? I tell you I don't know why I was sent there."

"All I hope is they believe you in England when you get home. And now you're back here, what d'you think you're going to do?"

"Run the canteen with Newcomb again, and see how much I can help the camp."

"Suppose the Prince won't let you go back to your old job?"

"Don't worry about that. He'll agree to whatever I want."

From then on the air in Room 3 was icy. I knew that unless I made other friends in the camp I would be very much on my own.

To my delight I found that regular church services were still being held, now taken by two New Zealand medical orderlies, Ian Ryburn and Win Giffen. Ian was a lay preacher back home, and would have been ordained but for the war. He was a wonderful man, and had a beneficial influence in the camp. I also heard that a Roman Catholic padre—Charbonneau—had arrived in the new English P.O.W. camp—Bau Battalion 21, next to E/3.

I found myself drawn more and more to Jim Newcomb and the New Zealanders. Day after day I spent hours playing bridge with Ian, Win and another fine "Kiwi", Tony Abraham. At night in the canteen I carried on with my secret service work, with Newcomb never asking a single question but ever on the alert lest the Germans would suddenly appear. I used Room 3 only for eating and sleeping for I knew that, although this was resented by the others, if I stayed there too much we would only start quarrelling. Otto put it bluntly, "Busty, we believe you, but it's the crowd at the back!"

John Borrie and I became particularly good friends. We made many of his medical trips together. We found we could obtain all sorts of equipment—financed through my canteen—for what was now a fine camp hospital, thanks to the good work of John and his medical orderlies. John and I went on trips further afield to Cosel, Gleiwitz, Kattowitz and Breslau, and had great fun smuggling various articles—especially musical instruments—back into the camp. His immunity as a doctor helped, while my friendliness with the Prince was good enough for the guards. Deep down John may have had suspicions of my activities, but he never let them show. We had a further bond in the organizing of concerts and religious services.

At this time there was a feeling of depression over the camp. Though the gigantic claims made by the German radio were not believed, the men knew from our own radio bulletins put out by Fred Neeve that Tobruk had fallen, Dieppe was a disaster, that the Germans were far into Russia, and that Stalingrad was in grave danger. The Japs were advancing on all fronts, and now Rommel was taking his Afrika Korps towards Egypt. The one grain of comfort was that at long last the R.A.F. were making severe raids on north-east Germany. It was understandable that a few British P.O.W.s who had lost everything—homes, wives or sweethearts—were thinking of going over to the Nazi side.

Barbed-wire mentality was a very real thing; and it became natural to suspect one who had too much truck with the Germans. It was known I was back in favour with Prince Hohenlohe and Paymaster Brauner. Many harsh things were said about my obvious pro-German attitude; it never seemed to occur to the accusers that I was risking my neck for camp welfare and therefore them.

One day Ian Ryburn came to me and said he was very worried about "goings on" at the far end of the camp. He took me along and I saw a dozen men lounging about near the entrance to an air-raid shelter which had recently been built near our football field.

"There's a girl down there, and these fellows are waiting their turn. She gets in under the wire when the German guard is round the other side. She's only about sixteen, and is given a bar of chocolate by each man."

"I think Dr Borrie ought to know about this. There could be a danger of V.D."

"I'm not only worried about disease, but about the Christian and mental state of our men."

The girl was later picked up by the Werkschutz outside the camp, and twenty chocolate bars were found on her—a busy day's pay. We found out afterwards that she had become mentally deranged and had been placed in a home.

Worse was to follow when the brothel for foreign workers duly opened across the canal. Our men soon sampled the pleasures there. Each day a number of them would leave the Baustelle and swim the canal, then swim back again satisfied. Those who could not swim had to make a long detour to get to the brothel. It was certainly well patronized.

A neighbouring camp had a German guard very much open to bribery. To save fellows the trouble of breaking through the wire he would let them out by the side of the sentry box. This worked well until the day the guard was arrested and taken away.

There was even a guard who fetched his two daughters along to amuse the men at work. When he found the demand was greater than he expected, he even volunteered to bring his wife too. The Germans were discovering that all the military successes they heard about were not bringing them any more clothes to wear or food to eat, so they were willing to degrade themselves in any way to get hold of some of the good things from the Red Cross parcels, or to augment their own meagre cigarette ration.

As the year wore on, the dentists left, Noakes to go to Sagan and Warren to Marlag Milag Nord. In their place came Julius Green, who was a Glasgow Jew. The Germans questioned him about his birth, but he was quick to deny he was a Jew, and the Germans then seemed satisfied. He came to live with us in Room 3, and it was obvious from the start that what little peace we enjoyed there was to be shattered, for "friend Julius" was just like a bull in a china shop; even the sergeant-majors seemed shocked at his behaviour.

Christmas was upon us, and this year there was plenty of food, with extra Red Cross parcels, and the men were in high good humour, each room having brewed a sufficient quantity of wine.

Julius Green claimed to be a fair expert on contract bridge, as I did myself; and it did not take me long to find out that when a game of bridge was suggested in our room, the best place for me was in the canteen. Julius was downright rude to the Germans, and set out to hurt any of them at his mercy in the dentist's chair. Even our own men, if they fell foul of Julius, took care to keep away from him in his official role until his wrath had subsided.

As time went on, the arguments did not end at the bridge table and Julius carried on day and night. He certainly got steamed up in the cubicle he shared with John Borrie, now divided off from the main room.

Then Julius started talking in a different manner, and I became seriously disquieted, for I realized that he too was working for Britain on secret service matters. What was particularly worrying was that his identification mark was identical to mine, which meant that should his talk get back to the Germans, I would be in grave danger. One day in early 1943 Julius actually explained the whole system to me. I acted of course as if I knew nothing about it, but it was obvious the whole scheme was liable to be sabotaged with so much talk, so I passed on the warning to England.

There was now no need at all for me to be in the area, and for my own peace of mind I decided it might be better for me to move. Even all the blackmarketing we were doing would be in safe hands with Julius.

In the spring of 1943, the B.B.C. gave us much better news on all fronts: we were winning in Africa—the magic of Rommel was now only a myth. The Japs were at last feeling the might of the combined American and Commonwealth forces; and in the air we were gaining superiority. After their defeat at Stalingrad when General Paulus and his entire Sixth Army fell to the Russians, the Germans were rapidly retreating. Camp morale rose higher than ever. But the Germans took the air attacks badly. In their wrath they turned on the slave workers, and atrocities increased. The Jews were worked until they could stand no longer, then taken to the gas chambers. If they did the slightest thing to annoy the Germans they were flogged unmercifully by one of their own community forced to carry out the punishment. Occasionally, as we passed the near-by Jewish camps, we saw Jews and others hanged for some trivial offence. I saw a Jew get up from his job, sway and stumble on the road which was just being surfaced. A steam roller was approaching, and before any of us could react what life was left in the body was crushed.

Then in the Russian P.O.W. camps near us the men were so ill-fed that hundreds were dying. Slowly our crime dossier was growing, each incident recorded for reference and punishment after the war—that is if we were lucky enough to live and put our evidence into proper hands.

In March 1943 a message arrived from England which made it imperative for me to return to Berlin as soon as possible. "Get full details of Englishmen broadcasting for the Germans. Let us have this as soon as possible." That evening I went to Newcomb in the canteen and told him I must get away.

"Well, Quarter, I reckon you're just wasting your time here, especially with that silly fool Julius blowing his head off all round the bloody camp."

"The problem is how to get back to Berlin. Can you think of a way?"

"Why not go back to your room, tell Julius and the others exactly what you think of them, get them all rowing with you, then tell the Prince they are making it impossible for you to stay here in Blechhammer? You're so well in with him, he'll believe you."

We duly had a terrific bust-up in Room 3, and I approached the Prince. He had heard about the row and readily agreed to my request.

"I will get in touch with the authorities in Lamsdorf and tell them what has happened. I am quite sure they can find you a job of some sort in Berlin. Would you be willing to work for *The Camp* newspaper if necessary?"

"I don't mind what I have to do as long as I get away from here."

"But you must be extremely careful what you do, for there are many in this camp who say you are too friendly with us. If you go to Berlin and do not come back here, many will return to England and say that you went over to the German side."

"That does not alter my desire to get to Berlin, or at least as far away from here as possible."

The Prince assured me that he would do his best. When I told him I would miss the friendship he had shown me, he said he was to be posted away from E/3 within the next few months; the Kommandant of the camp next door and several of the works chiefs had complained to Berlin that he was far too lenient with us. He thought he would be sent to Italy—but for his bad leg it would have been Russia. He spoke both languages fluently.

"There is nothing to worry about, for I know I am in no danger; there is nothing they can prove against me, except that I have tried to enforce the Geneva Convention as fairly and as humanely as possible. And if any action is taken against me, the international representatives of the Protecting Power will have something to say about it in Berlin."

"Perhaps it will be possible for us to meet in Berlin, or if not there, then in England when the war is over."

"You mean when our country is completely crushed to the ground because of the folly of our leaders?"

There was nothing more for me to say so I returned into the main camp, anxiously awaiting a message from Lamsdorf which would send me speeding once more to Berlin. Had I known what narrow shaves I was going to have before my work was finished, perhaps I would not have been so eager to make the journey again.

Meanwhile, the Abwehr (military intelligence) organized

several big raids on E/3. The Germans were getting more and more angry whenever the workers gave a Churchill V sign, or laughed at the German news bulletins, or even said they knew that something was *not* true—as they had heard the B.B.C. news from the British P.O.W.s. As usual we had advance warning and lost little, but one day Fred Neeve came into the canteen when I was alone.

"You know, Busty, I'm getting very worried about the radio. There's always the danger the Abwehr will find it in one of their raids. D'you think it would be possible for you to buy another set to have in reserve in case we lose this one?"

"I could no doubt make the necessary contacts outside, but I don't think we'll find it as easy to get it inside as the other one now that things are tightening up. Besides, in view of what's said about me in Room 3 and elsewhere, why the hell should I take the risk for the camp?"

"You're not doing it just for the camp, John. Just try to think what those poor wretches outside would feel like if they still believed what the lying swine are putting out on their radio. In any case you know full well I've never said anything against you, and rely on you whenever I want anything."

As usual the camp came before my own feelings. My contact was in one of the German canteens; the cook there said he was willing to sell me a radio set for 500 marks, three bars of chocolate and 500 English cigarettes. It was a pretty stiff price, but the goods were easily available, so I agreed to his terms. He asked how I proposed getting the set into the camp.

"The beer lorry with our men working on it calls here, doesn't it?" I said. "I'll have to bribe the driver. Once we get the set on to the lorry, it's no longer your responsibility. If anything goes wrong, say that the set was stolen from your office so that no suspicion falls on you."

"When will you have the set collected?" he asked.

"Next Wednesday without fail."

"Right you are then. Won't it be nice for you to hear the English news!"

"Yes, indeed."

"But the radio they're searching for so frantically is hidden in your camp?" he persisted.

"If it was, we'd hardly be wanting this one, would we?" I smiled.

That evening I sent for the corporal in charge of the camp workers and told him that on the following Wednesday I wanted four picked men to go out on the beer waggon, and explained what they had to do.

"I'd like to take charge of this myself, Quarter, if possible," said Hurley, Gloucester Regiment corporal.

"I was hoping you'd say that," I replied, "and I'd like you to take Jimmy Newcomb, Phil Kirby, and one other."

"How d'you think we can get the set in past the guards?"

"As a general rule you're not stopped when you come off the beer waggon, so we must just hope for the best. Of course, as soon as I hear you coming along, I'll go over and start chattering to the guards in my pro-German manner."

"O.K., Quarter, if you say it can be done, it will be done. Where shall we bring the set once we get inside the wire?"

"The best thing's to take it to your own room, and we can collect it after dark."

Wednesday came, and as soon as the beer lorry appeared, our four picked men went out. There was never any check on these men, as it was recognized that any member of the camp staff or any of the sick could go out for what the Germans considered to be a joy ride. I knew that the men would not be back before three o'clock, so I tried to busy myself to fill in the time. Then at about eleven o'clock the blow fell. The Prince sent for Sergeant-Major Haberfield and told him that the Protecting Power representatives were in the area, and would be making a visit at three o'clock that day. This meant the guards would be on their toes to make sure the camp was in order, but worse still both the Paymaster and the Prince would be back early; from their offices they had a clear view of the men coming in the gate, so the guards would be more vigilant than ever at this checkpoint. We could do nothing about it; certain disaster lay ahead. What worried me most of all was that four of our best men were involved, and there was no telling what the Germans would do to them in their anger.

The Protecting Power representatives duly arrived and went straight to the Prince's room. Immediately a German Gefreiter came round to inspect every room. He said there would be a special check at the gate so that nothing was brought in to make the rooms untidy. Then I heard the beer lorry stop at the gate, and with a thumping heart saw our four men coming down the pathway, one of them carrying a bulky object underneath his greatcoat. I could not go over to the guards to distract their attention. On State occasions like this the camp gates were out of bounds.

The Prince came out of his office in the company of the two Protecting Power representatives, and they walked towards the gate. I could see that the radio party and the Prince's party would meet there. As our boys marched unflinching on, the Gloucester corporal suddenly called, "Party, eyes left" and gave the Prince a perfect salute. The Prince, highly pleased at such military bearing, returned the salute and the guards swung open the gate. Our men marched through. In a moment they had passed us and had disappeared while we all went forward to greet our guests.

Our worries were not quite over, for the next thing we saw was the German Gefreiter running into the camp and making a beeline for the men's room. I followed and met him on his way out. He said he had wanted to make sure the men did not fling their coats about and make the room untidy.

"Did you find everything in order?" I asked innocently.

"Yes, they are very good fellows. They have put everything away, and the room looks very neat."

"That's good. Here, take a few cigarettes for yourself."

"Thank you very much, Herr Brown."

Thank God, it was all over. The miracle I had prayed for had happened again. For once I was favoured in Room 3.

At about that time the German authorities were becoming concerned at the number of men in our camp hospital. A German doctor who investigated found to his amazement that over a dozen prisoners had been recently circumcized by John Borrie. He could not understand why such an operation was necessary when the men were not Jewish, and were so completely cut off from all women. Up to this time the Germans had been assured of finding their Jewish victims by their one distinctive cut; but Borrie's operation spoiled all that! Further, the men had two weeks' rest till their circular wounds healed.

During my first three years of prison life I had managed to avoid hospital, although several times I had been laid low with fibrositis and had cursed the Germans for giving us wet grass as a bed in that terrible march of 1940. One day, however, I was walking into Room 3 when, without warning, I collapsed and was rushed into the camp hospital, apparently suffering from over-strain. For two weeks I took little interest in life. But Win Giffen, Corporal Cox and Ian Ryburn were wonderful nurses.

I had been convalescing for just a few days when I was summoned to the Prince, "You're leaving for Berlin tomorrow and this time will take all kit with you. Be as careful as you can," he said as I took my leave. "I'm quite sure the security people in Berlin have their doubts about you and I would not like to see you in trouble with them, nor would I like you to do anything against your own authorities."

I gathered that the Prince knew his own people would be utterly ruthless should I fall foul of them; but what was more interesting was the second part of his remark which indicated that my pro-German guise had deceived even so shrewd and well-informed an observer as Prince Waldemar of Hohenlohe.

Apart from several air raids on the way, the journey to Berlin was uneventful. On arriving there the first thing to strike me was the way the population were preparing for the severe air attacks which threatened them. There were now huge stone shelters and A.R.P. activity in evidence everywhere. The people it seemed had lost faith in Goering's oft-repeated assurance, "Bombs will never fall on the Reich". Buildings near Stalag IIID were damaged from recent raids.

When I entered the Stalag I was at once greeted by Major Heimpel, who shook me by the hand as though I were his long-lost friend.

"I'm very pleased to see you here again, Herr Brown, and I must apologize for the error which caused me to send you away last year."

"What I am more interested in, Major Heimpel, is why I was brought here the first time."

"I cannot give you a clear answer to that question, but at least I am able to tell you why you are here this time. The German High Command has decided that certain British prisoners have been working very hard for the Third Reich. They are to be invited to come to Berlin for a rest. In addition we hope to have a few prisoners who have found favour with the various Camp Kommandants in Germany."

"Are you quite sure it is not to be a political camp?"

"Of course not, Herr Brown. We want to break down the feeling of prejudice against the German nation, and especially against the Nazi Party."

"I will run the camp for you, Major Heimpel."

Joyce, it seemed, had reported back to them on my dumbness, and I was expected to run this camp without asking any questions. They also mistakenly assumed only officers were considered intelligent enough to be employed on secret service work, and were therefore foolishly locking them all up. Other ranks meanwhile, who were not restricted and were forced to go out to work, were picking up much valuable information and passing it on to England.

God alone knew what political tricks would be tried in the camp, for it was obvious the Germans were not going to give some hundreds of British prisoners a holiday unless the Führer stood to gain something from it. Whatever that something was I had quickly to discover.

That night I sat down and thought the whole matter out. I realized that if all went well, Heimpel had played completely into our hands. Here was my golden opportunity to make this camp the P.O.W. espionage centre in Germany. The men would come in from camps all over the Reich, would eventually return to them, and a network could be forged. Perhaps one could get escape kit to camps where no such articles were available. If I could gain a certain amount of freedom, I could carry out my special tasks, using the camp as excellent cover. I would need my own staff to run the camp my way. But utmost caution was needed. So far as Heimpel was concerned I would act absolutely dumb: he would get his "holiday camp" and, God willing, it would be quite different from what he expected.

The next day guards took me down to the new camp ten miles south of Berlin, near a village called Genshagen. Little did I know that the name would become famous—and infamous—throughout the P.O.W. camps in Germany. The nearest station, Grossburen, was a mile away. Beside it was a large field which showed signs of having been trampled on by people in heavy boots. I noticed that many people in working clothes left the train at the same time as we did, and that they went into a small building on one side of the railway line. I was puzzled by how so many could squeeze into such a tiny building and mentioned it to the guard. He said the building was all that could be seen of a vast underground tank factory. Experts claimed it was bomb-proof. My special work was piling up already.

Another point that struck me was that Genshagen was well within bombing range of the Berlin raiders, and if the Allies ever learnt about the Tiger tank factory, it could become very uncomfortable inside our own camp. However, we would have to put up with that!

The camp was in the middle of a forest and the vista was pleasant enough, though after so long in Germany one had tired of seeing pine trees. There were eighteen rooms, a first-class wash-house system, and an excellent concert hall, enclosed by barbed wire as a separate compound. The huts were close to the perimeter, and the centre of the compound would have been useful as a football pitch but had been dug up for crucial air-raid trenches. Outside was another piece of ground available for soccer or rugby football. The Germans had installed some camp staff, and a motley crew they were! In front of them I naturally kept up my pro-German guise and I could tell my attitude disarmed them. I soon discovered that half of them professed to be members of the British Union of Fascists, while the others had in some way found favour with the Germans. But try as I would I could not discover what was intended once the camp really got going. One member of the staff, a New Zealander, was making frequent trips out of camp, and it was rumoured that the first contingent of holidaymakers would soon be arriving.

One morning the German in charge, Sonderführer Lange who was well known to the Lamsdorf prisoners as "Canadian Joe", called me over to see him. I was confronted with an S.S. sergeant who sat dumb while Lange and I conversed in English. There was something about him which made me highly suspicious. When Lange went out of the room, leaving the S.S. man and myself together, the long silence was broken only when I said in bad German, "Can you speak any English?"

"Only a very little," came the reply in perfect German. Then Lange returned and I asked him what the S.S. man was doing in the camp. Lange said that when he had last been in his native village, he had found that one half of his home had been converted into a hospital. It was there that he found the S.S. man, Thomas Böttcher, recovering from a foot injury received in Russia. Later Böttcher had looked him up in Berlin. I listened carefully to all that was said, both between Lange and myself in English, and between Böttcher and Lange in German; but although I could not put my finger on what was wrong, I could not get out of my mind that there was something very strange about Böttcher.

Later, back in my room, it suddenly struck me. Of course, Böttcher was German for "Cooper", so perhaps our friend's name was Thomas Cooper. The next morning as I was having breakfast he walked into the room.

"Would you like a cup of good English tea?" I said to him in German.

"Yes please," he said with great gusto, "that is, if you can spare it."

I thought he seemed very eager at the mention of English tea, and when I handed him the cup I said, "Now that you are in Germany, I suppose you miss your English tea and cigarettes?"

He looked at me for a moment, and then said in perfect Cockney, "Well, it hasn't taken you long to guess my secret. I'm English all right, and my parents live in London."

"Then how did you get into the German Army, especially into the Waffen S.S.?"

"Oh, it's usual for the Germans to put all foreigners into the S.S."

"But what are you doing in the German Army at all?" I insisted.

"Well, my father's English and my mother German. I was on holiday in Germany when the war broke out, so I decided to take up German nationality. Because I was of military age I couldn't get a job, so I joined the army."

"Are you in sympathy with the Nazis?"

"Course I am. So'd you be if you'd had a job like mine in London. There I was earning fifty bob a week for some bloody Jewish timber merchants; and with no sign of promotion, I joined the Fascist Party. I took part in several meetings in the East End and had the satisfaction of helping smash up a few Jewish shops."

"What are you doing in this camp now?"

"I came here for a short holiday, but I'm hoping to get a job on the staff."

"Doing what?"

"That I can't say at the moment. But when you do find out, I hope you'll be willing to help me."

I noticed that Tom Cooper was on good terms with members of the camp staff, and frequently took them out. Where they went was always shrouded in mystery. One with whom Cooper was very friendly was a youngster named Oscar England—who told me he came from Bournemouth. I tried to find out from him what was going on; but he was extremely cagey about the whole business, although he admitted that the Germans were trying hard to get him to work for them. Then one day Oscar was taken seriously ill, and the German doctor told me he was not expected to live. I sat by his bedside for several nights, but he was too weak even to talk to me. Finally one night he suddenly sat up in bed and clutched my arm.

"John, I believe I'm very ill and will probably die, so I want you to know what's going on here. I want you to listen because you've been very decent while I've been ill."

"Take it easy, old man, don't overdo it."

"D'you realize most of us on the staff are either British Fascists, or violently anti-British?"

"Yes, I had noticed, but what's that got to do with it?"

"Well, we've been going into Berlin to meet some high officials of the German Foreign Office, and it's their intention to start a British Free Corps for blokes like us with anti-British, anti-Bolshevik feelings."

"And what advantage are you going to get out of it?"

"Well, because we were first in the Corps, we'd become officers and get the plum jobs."

"D'you mean to tell me that you're willing to go about in a German uniform, and S.S. at that?"

"Why shouldn't I? It means I'd have freedom to go where I please, and get any woman I want; and in any case we're going to have different badges to the ordinary Waffen S.S. Everybody'll be able to see we're English. Our shoulder flashes will read 'British Free Corps' and that above a Union

Jack. Instead of the S.S. flashes on the lapels, there'll be lions from the Royal Standard."

I asked how big the organization was, and he said that the only members were here in Genshagen. He proceeded to tell me who they were, and I made a careful note in my mind of all the names.

Then Oscar fell asleep, and I was left alone with my thoughts. Now I knew what villainous plan was in the minds of the Germans. But I would let them think I was still ignorant of it, for that seemed the best way to sabotage the whole thing.

Immediately I sent the news to England, and with it the names of the prisoners Oscar had said were willing to become members. I also enquired what I was to do about running such a camp. The reply came swiftly, "Congratulations on your startling information. You must carry on. Get all information, including names and numbers of suborned British P.O.W.s and without fail you must sabotage the whole thing."

Simple enough for them, so long as the Gestapo didn't catch me!

# 8

## *The Nazi "Holiday Camp"*

A few days later, when Cooper came and said I was to go with him to the German Foreign Office, I'd made up my mind what line to take.

We went by underground train to Potsdamer Platz, and were soon in the wonderful Chancellery building. I was ushered into a splendid room where I was introduced to a Dr Hesse and a Dr Ziegfeld. Dr Hesse told me he had been attached to the German Embassy in London before the war; and I later learned he was on Hitler's personal staff. Ziegfeld would be responsible to the German Foreign Office for Genshagen Camp.

"Mr Brown," Dr Hesse began, "we understand from our military authorities that you have been a most reasonable prisoner. You have been selected by us to run a special camp, the first of its kind in Germany. We feel the time has now come for a better English understanding of German policy, so that when we've won the war Englishmen will be more ready to co-operate with us in the struggle against communism."

"If this is to be a political camp I wish to have nothing whatever to do with it!"

"You can rest assured on that point, Mr Brown. You will in no way be compromised, for we intend that you should be in charge of a genuine holiday camp. You should feel very honoured to be chosen. We have brought you here today to discuss the matter fully, and see if you have any ideas on how to run the camp."

"What type of entertainment do you have in mind?"

"We hope to get the pick of the German artistes available in Berlin; and to make sure that nothing political is attempted we want you to meet each artiste beforehand and discuss his or her programme."

Captain Julius Green, Army Dental Corps, at Blechhammer in 1943

The room in Stalag IIID in which Brown stayed during his first trip to Berlin

John Brown (*left*) in costume at one of the many shows put on at Genshagen

The camp orchestra at Genshagen

"How often will these people be available?"

"Probably once a week."

"Then I suggest that we get in touch with the Y.M.C.A. to see if a talkie apparatus can be obtained with films, and also as much sports and games equipment as we can get."

There was an awkward silence for a moment, then Dr Ziegfeld said, "For the present we do not wish to have people outside know about the camp."

"But if it is to be a genuine camp, surely there is nothing to hide—in fact exactly the reverse."

"Very well then, the Y.M.C.A. can be contacted."

"And I think that in a camp of this nature a strong religious side is most important."

"That is entirely up to you—we have nothing to say either way about that."

"I think too we ought to have a permanent staff capable of providing good plays, and also have visits of dance and military bands from the other camps, so that we can give a show every night."

"We are willing to agree to whatever you say. Can you tell us for certain now that you are willing to help us, or are we to send you away? Of course, you cannot go back to Prince Hohenlohe at Blechhammer, for he is now in Italy; and in any case we would not like to have our plans discussed. So it would be necessary to send you somewhere away from other prisoners."

What a pleasant little threat, I thought; but I had to keep my temper, because if I played my cards correctly I could probably get all I wanted—so long as they thought I knew nothing of the British Free Corps scheme.

"I *am* willing to co-operate with you provided I can get my own staff to run the camp."

"Are you not satisfied with the men already there?"

"They would not be of any use to me for entertainment or sports purposes."

Hesse and Ziegfeld hastily conferred in whispers. Then Hesse said to me, "We are willing to let you have your own staff, but now we must impose a special condition on you. We do not wish you to feel uncomfortable when you are with the German artistes in Berlin, so it is our desire that you should wear civilian clothes when you meet them."

I could hardly believe my ears; this was too good to be

true, though their intention was all too obvious: to compromise me from the very beginning. Whatever happened, I had to be careful not to appear over-eager.

"But it would be quite impossible for me to wear civilian clothes within the camp."

Dr Hesse smiled slightly. "You think your men might feel you are working on the German side?"

"It would destroy the idea of the camp being run straight without any attempt at propaganda."

"Yes, we think you are quite right; and to cover yourself when you are alone in Berlin, we will give you an Ausweis which will be very useful to you. It will say that because you are friendly towards German politics you must be given every consideration, and when shopping must have every priority. It will mean that you will practically have the freedom of Berlin and be able to go where you will and meet whomever you wish, including women. We hope you will enjoy yourself, especially with the women; but do not of course take liberties."

Did I detect a faint threat in his last words? "Such a passport will be very useful," I replied, "for I'll need to buy a lot of goods for the camp canteen. You may rest assured I will make the best use of it."

Dr Hesse thanked me and the interview was over, the Germans probably congratulating themselves at finding such a simpleton to run the camp, and thinking what a fine cover they had for bringing in their prospective British Free Corps members. On my side I reckoned that with my own staff I would be able to keep a tight grip on what was going on, and I would have an excellent opportunity to card-index every prisoner coming to the camp so that, should any of them go over to the Germans, I had all the information required by England. And my plan to have an espionage network all over Germany was becoming a distinct possibility. Before long all the camps could be warned of the Free Corps plan, and all the likely Quislings watched and gently persuaded to be sensible, though this would have to be done discreetly so as not to alert the Germans. In this way the failure of the Free Corps could be regarded almost as a certainty. The only snag was that almost all the prisoners would regard the holiday camp as a German propaganda centre and we might as a result get all kinds of amateur nosey parkers investigating and so destroying a lot of care-fully thought out work. But I would have to put up with that.

A more immediate problem was what to do with Tom Cooper? He would need watching twenty-four hours a day. I thought the best plan was to make friends with him, and let him come more or less freely into our room. Then, when he went into other rooms or when I was out on business, I would have to get one of my trusted staff to watch him. It was like neutralizing the sting of a very dangerous fly—and funnily enough he looked rather like one. In a way I felt sorry for him with his mixed parentage; he was just another of those who had not been given a fair chance in pre-war England.

During one of our talks I asked him what was going to happen to England when Germany had won the war.

"We'll just make a little garden city out of the place. All being well, I hope to become a Gauleiter over there, and to meet some of the swine who made me work for next to nothing." He considered the war all but won, and went on to say that shortly the new German weapons would be launched on England "with devastating effect". But though I pressed him for details he pleaded ignorance. He was just an immature boy trying to behave like a grown-up: but what a dangerous bugger to have around a camp like Genshagen!

The Holiday Camp started in June 1943, and it soon became suspect among most P.O.W.s, simply because we were unable to say what we were doing there. And of course although I was able to have my own staff, they were not aware of my outside activities but trusted me implicitly. They were not even worried when we heard a question had been asked in Parliament about the "propaganda camp known as Genshagen". No doubt the authorities had ac-curate information about it!

By the time I had finished gathering in my picked staff around me I had an excellent espionage ring established within the camp itself. First of all I got Jimmy Newcomb from Blechhammer to run the canteen, thus ensuring that we would be able to get everything into the camp which was strictly forbidden. Next came Ian Ryburn to run the reli-gious side, for I felt the genuine holidaymaker would go back with a better feeling within after he had come into contact with Ian. Then I found good men to run the hospital, the entertainments, shoe-repairing, tailoring and such like until we had no weak link in the chain. The doubtful ones were split up around the camp, and my staff took good care to see they kept out of mischief. It was strange to see how certain of these fellows were always singled out for special notice when any high-ranking German military gentleman came to visit the "wonderful new camp".

At first the Germans, with their meticulous love of detail, were for ever demanding reports of our activities; the camp was even mentioned in their newspapers, though of course nothing was said as yet about the Free Corps—the Nazis wanted to be assured of success before broadcasting their latest little bit of villainy.

The office work was so time-consuming that I decided to get an old friend from Blechhammer to do it for me. I could not have hoped for a better German-hater for such work than Reginald Beattie. In the old days he had argued with me that Germany could not last out 1940; but now he agreed he had been over-optimistic. His three years in captivity had mellowed him, but strengthened more than ever his belief that victory for Britain was certain. I put him in charge of our camp intelligence, and from this time onwards I was able to forget all about this most important side of my work. Beattie had a flare for "smelling out" pro-German prisoners and he was assisted by a very able New Zealander, Tony Abraham. Beattie found it hard to be polite at all to the Germans, but for the sake of his job he did his best to sink his personal feelings. Many times I saw him gritting his teeth and glowering at the Germans and their cocksure acceptance that within a few months Britain would be crying out for mercy. It was strange how all the Germans were utterly confident of the effectiveness of the new weapons Hitler was brewing up; and yet nobody seemed to know what they were.

After Beattie had nosed out any prisoners who appeared tainted with the Nazi brush he would report to me, and then our little organization would go to work in a roundabout way. I kept in the background, but should my staff find it impossible to dissuade someone from the traitor's path, I would then take what action I considered necessary. Sometimes I would sow a grain of suspicion in the ear of the Germans, suggesting that the man in question was trying to double-cross them; he was known to us as Communist and it was obvious he had come to the camp only to wreck the good feelings the Germans were trying to foster. My stock with the Sonderführer rose, while several pro-German P.O.W.s found themselves in punishment camps for the rest of the war. But to my mind that was much better than joining the British Free Corps and, were they to survive that, then facing a treason trial should they ever return to England. Several times the Germans tried to wangle one of their favourites on to my staff; but our simple espionage check-up was very efficient in nosing out such attempts.

The first group of prisoners who arrived in June stayed till the end of August. They were able to see the various sights and buildings of Berlin which had so far escaped air-raid damage. Organization of free time proved to be somewhat difficult, and shows were not provided as I had intended. It was just like the Germans to start a recreation camp of this nature, yet not give us a single item of sports equipment or even games. Supplies from the Y.M.C.A. were naturally very slow in coming through and at first they were suspicious of it. It did not take me long to realize that the camp could only be as successful as I made it for, although the Nazis were only too willing to reap their own advantage from Genshagen, they were not prepared to put themselves out to provide proper cover for their nefarious purpose.

The first batch of prisoners who went back to the coal mines and quarries and other back-breaking work of Silesia had at least had six weeks' good rest, and most of them left clothed in decent battledress and overcoat, and a good pair of boots. Some indeed had arrived at Genshagen still wearing the clothes they had been captured in three years before. It was easy for the Germans to give us this new clothing: under the direction of Major Heimpel it had been stolen from Red Cross supplies—presumably intended for German paratroopers to use when they invaded England. If it made the British P.O.W.s feel a little better disposed towards the Führer, why not let them have some of what they were entitled to anyway?

When the camp broke up on the morning of 31st August 1943, my staff felt that at least they could have a breather before the next party arrived. But it was not to be. That night the R.A.F. paid us a visit—the fearful forerunner of almost two hundred major raids, both day and night, that we endured before the camp finally closed. Most staff had gone to bed when the alarm went; but they were so used to the howling of the sirens that most stayed there. There had been numerous false alarms during the last two months when we had spent hours down in the trenches, wishfully thinking that it was in earnest, and that a few more Nazis were getting what they deserved.

But on this night the guns could be heard firing in the distance while the drone of the planes was quite distinct and getting louder and closer all the time. Most of the men began casually to dress. Then came the sound of bombs dropping: there was a rush for the shelter. The planes were overhead and the bombs crashing nearer and nearer while a circle of white lights appeared round the camp, as if the perimeter lights had become magnified a thousandfold. We looked at each other, knowing our chance of survival was in the lap of the gods. All hell broke loose.

Night became day, the glare of hundreds of searchlights augmenting the light of the flares around the camp. Bombs whistled through the air, but it was the one that would fail to whistle which we feared most. I stood with Newcomb fascinated, watching the terrible scene; but when a bomb landed just outside the wire, discretion seemed the better part of valour: we went below.

There we found some of the staff huddled in a corner while others, presumably more fatalistic, sat in a circle around a member playing the banjo, so that while the R.A.F. poured their rain of death from the skies, we could hear the strains of "There'll always be an England". I felt proud to be English. Then, as I looked towards the end of the trench and saw the seven men who I knew would shortly be leaving to form the nucleus of the British Free Corps, I felt sickened. There were these "brave fellows" willing to fight against England because they were, or said they were, in sympathy with the Nazi cause, at this moment crouched against the earthen wall of the shelter, terrorized because of the R.A.F. bombing.

Just then, with an unusually close and heavy crash, part of the shelter fell in—a part where fortunately no one was but would have been had the first group still been there. For the next five minutes bombs fell all around us: we could hear the crunch as the camp buildings vanished.

When we finally emerged, we found the bath-house ablaze. The Germans were attacking the flames as best they could. Overhead the planes were being picked up by search-lights, and ack-ack was exploding all around them. Some of our planes had been hit and were sinking ablaze to the ground, slowly and majestically. The Germans were un-merciful. If a plane was hit, perhaps in flames, ack-ack fire would concentrate on the crippled machine. Then in the glare of the searchlights we picked out parachutists and heard the rattle of machine guns and rifle fire as the poor devils fell within range. Nearby was a huge searchlight which seemed to provide a focus for all the other search-lights in the area. Then we heard the roar of a plane over-head and we watched fascinated as the airman flew straight down the beam of the searchlight. As the bomb fell there was a blinding flash and sudden darkness. The broad beam was put out for ever. Only a gaping hole remained where the searchlight had been, and the corpses of four men and three women in German uniform.

When the tumult had died down, I asked my staff to check whether we had any casualties. I was alarmed to find one man missing—Seaman Johnson. We searched the air-raid shelters for him while the wrecked end of one shelter was being dug out. Then we noticed that while practically all the rooms had been knocked into grotesque shapes, the one where Johnson slept was intact. There we found him fast asleep in bed. He said he had not heard the raid, and even if he had he would not have got up.

From the wreckage of the camp we realized how much hard work lay ahead before we could have another party of holidaymakers in.

But it was duly done, and by the time the camp opened for the second party we had been able to obtain a collection of useful articles from the Y.M.C.A. and organize a full pro-gramme so that something was on every night—a play, talking film, fancy-dress dance, or band show. During the day there were sporting activities, including swimming;

and as before, trips into Berlin. These walks in the city became a stimulant for our men now that the bombing was taking its toll, for when they returned to their own camps they relayed the news to the other prisoners. It served as a tonic to those who were shut off from civilization. Each time a party went into Berlin one of my trusted staff accompanied it, with orders to keep their eyes skinned for any information which might be of use.

In their wily manner the Germans tried to have us include some mild propaganda in our concert programme; but the holidaymakers were prepared for this and did not mind so long as they had plenty of English programmes. I was next asked by the Germans if we could arrange a weekly show at which the platform would be open to any prisoner who would like to recount any outstanding experience he had had in a P.O.W. camp, or any amusing or bizarre anecdote he could remember as a "Kriegie". At first the request sounded innocent enough; but the more I thought about it the less I liked it. What the Germans wanted was for some silly idiot to get on his feet and unwittingly betray some camp secret which the Germans had not been able to ferret out. As I did not want to let the Germans know I had seen through their scheme, I sent for a member of the staff and told him to organize such a show, but to make sure that each week some invented "secret" was leaked in order to lead the Germans even further up the garden path.

We had been given a few old German films, but they were of a non-provocative nature and had little chance of competing against the splendid English and American films which the Y.M.C.A. were providing and which enabled us to give two full-length shows each week.

The Germans seemed content for me to run the camp, and did not interfere greatly with our arrangements, doubtless happy to have the six or seven fellows working for them on behalf of the British Free Corps. I was confident that no others had joined them, so good was our counter-checking system by now. I felt happy to have established a genuine holiday camp at which prisoners from the coal mines and quarries were able to get six weeks of complete rest or, if they preferred, could have a hectic Butlins-type holiday, with plenty to eat and opportunities to meet women.

The Germans would delight in bringing famous artistes—singers, pianists, violinists, dancers, military bands and the like to the camp, primarily to show they were full of goodwill, but above all to prove their culture was so much better than our own. It must be said that some of their lectures were excellent, but all the time we felt they were trying to convince us that they belonged to a superior race. The prisoners lapped up the good music and singing and gained what they could from the lectures, but the other stuff left them cold.

It was Dr Ziegfeld who dealt with this side of the camp and I believe he tried to engage the most harmless people to talk to us, because he was keen on the idea of a genuine holiday camp without any of the dirty work the Germans had in mind.

One personality he brought was Max Schmeling, the world-famous boxer who we understood had been in trouble because he had swiped Goebbels a doughboy after the latter had tried to make love to Max's actress wife. The concert hall was filled to capacity when he arrived with Ziegfeld and he was loudly clapped as he walked on to the stage. There was another burst of clapping after Ziegfeld had introduced him, but Schmeling simply said, "Thank you very much", jumped off the stage, and sat down in the front row, demanding to know when the show was to start. It was only after some persuasion that he agreed to come back on stage and answer questions about his career in the ring. Afterwards when alone with me he said he had no time whatever for the Nazis, and that he had refused to speak at first because he thought he was being used for propaganda purposes. He was a shy, retiring man, and was most appreciative when we gave him some cigarettes and chocolate.

Another welcome visitor was a person introduced to me as Frau Strohm, for I soon discovered she was none other than the famous Wigan-born operatic singer Margery Booth who had been married to a German before the war and was a member of the Berlin State Opera. She sang in the camp and her rendering of old English folk songs brought tears to the eyes of many a hardened prisoner. But there was trouble when she tried to sing "Land of Hope and Glory" to conclude her programme. Ziegfeld had a difficult time trying to explain this away to the German High Command, for of course in their eyes Margery Booth was a full German and had no right whatever to sing patriotic English songs. I was extremely moved the first time I heard her sing, but I did not know then that I was to have to trust her implicitly.

The important religious side of the camp was prospering under the spiritual guidance of Ian Ryburn, who continued to live a saint-like life and be a shining example to the rest of the camp. One day one of the most fanatical of the British Free Corps probables came to me and said he would like to attend the services regularly and take a full part in the Christian life. My first thought was a very unchristian one— that he had been sent by the Germans so that he would wheedle his way into the church and make sure there was no anti-German talk coming from the pulpit (not that Ian of all people would do such a thing). But I was proved wrong since the nucleus of the British Free Corps eventually left the camp, the man stayed behind and in fact became a very useful member of my staff. There was no doubt that quite a number of would-be Free Corps members were deterred by the work done by Ian.

In the midst of all the intrigue and underhandedness around us, the "spirit of Genshagen" became a genuine thing. After four years of war, "barbed-wire madness" was inevitably on the increase and could only be controlled by a strong personality. Ian had that personality, and many of the prisoners who eventually got home owed it to the part Christian worship had played in their P.O.W. lives. It was a strange thing that in almost every camp somebody came forward to organize services, even if it meant writing out every hymn and taking the service from memory. But Ian Ryburn was a gift from heaven in our little community.

I spent hours with him discussing religious problems. My greatest relaxation after a hard day's snooping around in Berlin was to talk to him about our common faith. I was worried by the possible clash between my intelligence work and my Christian beliefs, for how could I reconcile passing on information, which might cause the deaths of hundreds of people, with loving one's enemies? But although I could not tell Ian about my special work, I gained from him the courage to carry on in the conviction that our cause was right.

As attendance at the little church grew, the need for a

parson who could officiate at Holy Communion increased. The Germans were reluctant to allow any of the many padres in the prison camps to visit Genshagen, either because they were still touchy about their prize camp, or because they feared that as the padres had officer rank they might be engaged on secret service work. I spoke to Ian about the need for a parson, convinced that he himself was more than ready to enter the ministry; and I suggested that the New Zealand church authorities should be approached in the matter. Ian agreed to this course, and I immediately contacted the Y.M.C.A. representative in Sagan, who in turn got in touch with the Geneva office. After a short delay permission came through from New Zealand for Ian to be ordained in Germany by one of the captured New Zealand padres, Padre Griffiths. Ian would have to complete his studies after the war, but for the duration he could minister to us.

For once the Germans co-operated with us in making arrangements for the ordination, and Chaplain Captain R. J. Griffiths arrived from the Lamsdorf area with authority to complete the laying on of hands. In a solemn and beautiful ceremony attended not only by practically every man in the camp, but by several high-ranking German officials from Berlin, Ian became a priest of the New Zealand Presbyterian Church.

The second party went away, and shortly afterwards we lost the nucleus of the British Free Corps. When I asked the Germans where these men had gone, I was told that they had been sent back to their original Stalags, but I knew that to be untrue. I heaved a sight of relief when I knew that we were at last free of the traitors. There was nothing more we could do to help them while they remained in the camp, and they were a real danger to all my schemes.

Cooper was still with us, but spent much time away from the camp. One day when he was a little tight on schnapps I had acquired through visiting artistes, I challenged him about this. He then let the cat out of the bag about the formation of the British Free Corps. Of course he told me nothing I did not already know except that the official announcement about it was to be made in January, 1944. He would then go with the original seven members recruiting round all camps in Germany. It was satisfying to know that

Britain was aware of this Corps at least four months before the German public.

As for Cooper and his satellites visiting the camps, being forewarned was as good as being forearmed; with just a little strategy we could give these gentlemen a very rough passage in their work. But there was one snag: supposing this new recruiting method meant that those with itchy feet would *not* come to Genshagen, but go straight to the Free Corps? That would do away with my chance to work on them and card-index them.

Tom assured me that the present arrangements would go on. Ziegfeld was so pleased with all the good things being said about Genshagen that he wanted to separate the Free Corps and the camp once and for all. This posed a pretty problem, for although I was very keen on my holiday camp I certainly did not want to lose my links with the Free Corps, or, through it, the German Foreign Office.

# 9

## *Free in Berlin*

With the holiday camp running so well, I felt I could pro-
fitably spend more time in Berlin which was obviously
bristling with information badly wanted in England. But to
get anywhere in the city I would have to look like a German
civilian. Realizing the risk, and knowing that if any P.O.W.
in Genshagen saw me in civvies my stock would fall even
lower, I approached Ziegfeld reminding him of his promise
of a civilian suit and Ausweis to cover me when out alone.
Ziegfeld put the matter to the German Foreign Office; but it
seemed they had got cold feet and were no longer keen for
me to wander alone. Behind their attitude I sensed the
smiling face of Heimpel who still had his doubts about me.

Then one morning I received a request from England
which made it imperative to have freedom of movement in
Berlin: "Verify the identity of John Amery". A simple
enough request, but how the devil could I contact the fellow
if I were confined behind barbed wire? And as the gentleman in question probably spent most of his time in the most
exclusive establishments in Berlin I could hardly approach
him with a German guard. I did feel the request itself was
unnecessary; surely England must know what the chap was
doing. But orders were orders. So I went at once to the
Foreign Office and told them that if they let me have a
civilian suit, I would be able to get much more for the
canteen and so improve camp life. I also pointed out that I
felt entitled to a little freedom in return for my work in
making the holiday camp a success. Desperate to get out, I
used every possible argument. The matter was referred to
the "England Kommittee", the Foreign Office Department
which dealt with propaganda to Britain and British
P.O.W.s. When I was called into the room Dr Hesse was in
the chair, and fortunately Ziegfeld was with him, for the

latter was as friendly to the British as he dared be. He was always trying to improve conditions in prison camps (I knew that it was through him that the handcuffing of some of our men which took place after the Dieppe raid in 1942 had been stopped). The third man in the room I recognized as Dr Seeberg, editor of the P.O.W. newspaper *The Camp*. I thought I could rely on him, for I had loaned him some of my camp staff to help repair his bomb-damaged house. I was greatly relieved that neither Joyce nor Heimpel were there.

"We have received your request to go out in civilian clothing," Dr Hesse began, "but we must have good reasons before we can think of granting such a request."

I reminded him of what he had said at our last meeting about requiring me to wear civilian clothes.

"Yes, but since then the Allied bombing has been intensified and we are afraid of spies in the city."

"Surely you are not suggesting that I would associate with spies? I'm running Genshagen for you."

"Of course not, Mr Brown, we trust you, but you must realize we have to be extremely careful."

"I would suggest you don't want to issue me with a pass simply because you are afraid of Major Heimpel."

This made Dr Hesse very angry, and he insisted he was responsible only to Hitler, and that Heimpel's only interest in Genshagen was the supply of guards.

Ziegfeld then spoke. "Don't you think your authorities in England would misunderstand if it were reported that you are going about freely in civilian clothes in Berlin?"

"That point hardly matters, Dr Ziegfeld, if we are to accept the belief that Germany will win the war."

Hesse brightened up considerably. "Why do you not ask us to give you a pass and make you into a civilian, away from any P.O.W. camp?" he asked.

"It would then be impossible for me to carry on with my Genshagen work in which I have a very keen interest."

"But what are the prisoners going to say when they see you walking about inside the camp in ordinary clothes?"

I agreed that was out of the question, and said I would have to take a suitcase out through the gates with me and change in a field.

My request was granted, and almost at once I received a well-made wool suit and a German Foreign Office pass which stated that I was a British prisoner politically favourable to Germany and was therefore allowed the freedom of Berlin in civilian clothes. And when making purchases I was to be treated with civility and given priority over German shoppers.

It must have been one of the very first occasions that a man in my position had been granted a pass to go out alone. My suit very quickly grew into three, for I found a tailor in Berlin who considered himself every bit as good as Savile Row. He was fond of coffee, while I wanted some of his pre-war suiting, so we made a deal, and he made me one of the best-dressed men in Berlin. Vanity made me regret I could not wear my suits openly for the whole camp to envy, but I had no desire to be branded a Nazi by all. It became a little irksome to have to change in the field, particularly when the weather turned so cold that even the proverbial brass monkey would have suffered emasculation—but I was not nearly as tough as it was! That night on my return from town, I found that my suitcase containing my army uniform had been stolen from the bushes where I had hidden it. I had to wait until darkness fell and then crept quietly into the camp.

It struck me that it was high time I discovered more about the secret Daimler-Benz tank factory, the entrance to which backed on to Genshagen railway station. I thought the factory, which was invisible from the air, would make a fine target for our bombers if only I could get ideas on the vulnerable points. But how to get inside?

Next morning I reported my lost uniform to Sonderführer Lange, and after stressing what a ruinous effect it would have on the camp if I were seen in civvies, I suggested changing in the Daimler-Benz factory. Much to my surprise he agreed, and next day made the necessary arrangements with the factory caretaker.

We became friends: he had a wife and children who loved chocolate, and he himself enjoyed coffee and English cigarettes. I was very liberal with gifts, and it was only natural that I should ask to see his wonderful factory. The caretaker was sorry he could not agree—each section of the factory was sealed off and an admission disc to each section was needed before entry was permitted. He showed me the numbered discs and the factory plan, setting out which disc was required for entry to which part. Before long he was telling me how the Tiger tanks left the factory each day, and how they came out of the "hill" by widely separated tunnels in order to deceive any aircraft which might be on the lookout. The caretaker was proud of the factory, which was indeed highly ingenious, and I was able to piece together a satisfactory plan of it and, in the caretaker's absence collect the various discs.

Not long after I had been right through the factory and sent news of vulnerable points to England, a series of heavy air raids in the area damaged it severely. My changing room was bombed out, which was a blow, for it meant returning to Jack Frost's parlour in the chilly fields.

Being within a mile of the factory our own camp was in grave danger, and when the raids came my heart was in my mouth. The American daylight raids with their pattern bombing were particularly frightening. They sought not only the target but much else surrounding it, so that our camp a mile away was much too close for comfort. The inevitable happened and the camp was again hit, this time wrecking the German quarters and one part of our barracks. When we examined our beds after the first raid we found holes going right through them where the incendiary bombs had penetrated. It was as well that the camp members were now shelter-minded, including Seaman Johnson who awakened remarkably quickly at the first wail of the siren and was now first into the shelter. In one of the first raids the ceiling of his little room had collapsed on him, and with some difficulty he was dug out of the wreckage.

Having gained some freedom, the breath of fresh air and the sight of so many charming women strutting about the streets of Berlin giving their Heil Hitler salute to passers-by, caused the sap to rise within me too. But before I strayed, I had first to establish the identity of John Amery.

That meant an introduction to the man. I knew he had written a book attacking the capitalists of England and prais-ing the Nazi ideology. I approached Tom Cooper and told him I wanted to talk to Amery about the book. Cooper was only too willing to arrange such a meeting, for it seemed that Amery also was interested in the British Free Corps. Cooper had still not tumbled to the fact that his efforts were being nullified by my most efficient staff. Rumours had

Margery Booth, the opera singer who helped John Brown in Berlin

The Café Vaterland, a night-club in Berlin which John Brown and Jimmy Newcomb used to frequent with Margery Booth

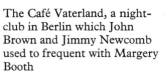

Thomas Cooper-Böttcher, who was a member of the Waffen S.S. and who was later tried at the Old Bailey, London, in 1946 on the charge of high treason

John Brown and a journalist fellow-prisoner interviewed by Lydia Oswald, a reporter on the *Swiss Illustrated*, at Genshagen reached me that some of the German top brass were dis-satisfied with the recruitment rate and that John Amery, who until this time had been looking for pro-Nazi types in the French prison camps, was to put the Free Corps on a sound footing and so confirm his undivided loyalty to the Führer. The meeting was arranged in the Hotel Adlon. Cooper and I were sitting in superb comfort when a rather short man in his early thirties arrived with a gaily dressed woman. I was introduced to Amery and his French wife. I had read in the German papers how his first wife had been found dead in bed, apparently suffocated with pillows; as the German coroner had put it, it was a clear case of accidental death, so very sad for Mr Amery! I could not help noticing that Amery smelt strongly of scent, and that his hands were perfectly manicured. His wife had some trace of the Eurasian in her, and although she was dressed very smartly, there was little left to the imagination.

Amery produced a couple of bottles of French brandy, the first I had seen for nearly four years. He said he had bought them cheaply on the black market in France.

"I was anxious to meet you," he continued, "as I've heard so much about you from Tom Cooper, Dr Hesse and several others."

"I hope what you heard was complimentary."

"Yes, except that Joyce doesn't seem to like you. But you needn't worry about that: he's probably jealous because you're so popular with the Germans."

"But I'd have thought he would have been a great friend of yours."

"No, our work is in quite different directions. I don't mind him so much, but I can't stand his wife with her foul language. Joyce wants to get in on the British Free Corps and obtain all the credit, but I'm not going to let him."

"What do you mean by the 'British Free Corps', Mr Amery? I'm afraid it doesn't mean anything to me."

"I'm sorry, I assumed you'd have been told about it before now. But it doesn't matter, as I'm sure once you do hear about it you will be only too pleased to co-operate with me."

"Is there a Free Corps already in existence?" I asked innocently.

"Yes, but no public announcement has yet been made. I

should say we have about two hundred in it at present."

Either he was a damned liar or my intelligence staff had slipped up badly; we figured less than thirty.* I asked Amery how many numbers he anticipated once the thing was working properly.

"My target is a minimum of five thousand ex-prisoners, and I am quite confident of getting that number very easily, as I told Himmler this morning."

I asked him how he intended recruiting so many.

"Those who are already members will go canvassing round the camps under the supervision of Tom Cooper, and once the prisoners realize what a wonderful time they will have outside, what with women and wine and the opportunity to work for our Führer, I'm sure the rush will be so great that we'll have to refuse applicants. Up to now, Genshagen has been used as a blind for the Free Corps, but I hope to separate the two schemes at once."

Once again I was a little saddened by this news, although a plan had formed in my mind which might overcome the difficulty. "I think it is wonderful," I said, "how you have been able to keep all this from me for so long."

Amery smiled in self-satisfaction at my remark. "You just watch out for the publicity we're going to give the Corps, and you will see at once I'm the right man to run the scheme. I told Himmler this morning it is my intention to turn what has been a near-failure into a resounding success. In fact 5,000 is a conservative estimate, and we can't go wrong."

"By the way, Mr Amery, will you allow me to congratulate you on the excellent book you have written?"

"Do you like it?"

"Yes, very much indeed."

"Has it been circulated in all P.O.W. camps?"

"As far as I know, yes; it is certainly available in Genshagen."

"What do the other prisoners think of it?"

"They like it too, but there seems to be some doubt in their minds as to whether John Amery really did write it. Many of them say it must have been written by a German."

---

* This was pretty near the mark. Thirty-odd was the number quoted at one of the Old Bailey treason trials after the war.

I saw Amery colour up at this remark, and I knew that the brandy must be taking its toll, as it was to some extent on me although I felt the conversation was going very nicely for me.

"But that's a bloody silly thing to say—ask Tom whether I wrote it or not."

"There is no need to do that, for I am perfectly convinced you wrote it. But don't you see, the book loses much of its value if those reading it are not entirely convinced you did write it."

"What can I do to overcome that?"

"Well, you would have to give them proof of your identity in some way."

"Well, see if that will satisfy the buggers!" At that he threw his British passport on to the table in front of me, and I knew my task was accomplished. I quickly memorized the number.

"Don't be foolish, Mr Amery," I said as I pushed the passport back to him, "it's not *me* you have to convince, it's the other prisoners."

The meeting ended soon after this, and Amery went away doubtless happy to know I was fully with him and satisfied as to his identity. So was I. When London got the information he would stand condemned. That night I was in high spirits, as was Tom Cooper who felt his prestige had gone up by bringing Amery and myself together. We went to the Café Vaterland together, and by the time we returned to Genshagen were both tired out and pleasantly plastered.

A few days later, I was there again entertaining Cooper, who was in civvies, and Sonderführer Meyer—Smokey Joe of Lamsdorf—who was in uniform. We were all smoking and drinking when a man in civilian clothing walked by, took Meyer's cigarette out of his mouth, and said in perfect English, "How nice to see a real Players again." Then he walked rapidly out of the room. The whole thing happened so quickly that he had gone before anybody moved. Meyer was frightened in case the man was a Gestapo agent, but I felt sure the man was trying to pass me a message.

Two days later I met him again when I was on my own. He disclosed to me that he was living as a civilian but working for England, and he wanted to warn me that, although I had apparent freedom, I was being closely followed wherever I went. He advised me that the best way to throw the watchers off the scent would be to find a girlfriend, and appear to give all my time to her. This would provide excuses for being out late at night and the Germans, who loved a bit of fun and believed in "strength through joy", would always turn a blind eye to such goings-on. His parting words were, "Don't forget, find a nice girl, for she may be useful to you more than physically. Should you ever meet me again in Berlin, ignore me completely unless I speak to you. Good luck in your work—you'll need it!" At that he left, with a Heil Hitler salute. He had my admiration as he went out into the night, for he was alone in this big city, while I at least could return to my little bit of England in Genshagen. I wondered how many more men were doing similar work alone.

By this time I had persuaded the dumb Germans to let me have a number of other civilian suits so that any member of staff going out of the camp could do so out of uniform. I argued that the heavy bombing of Berlin had so incensed the population that it was unsafe for our men to go into Berlin in uniform. Of course I intended the suits to be used by my most trusted men so that they could get around and pick up useful information. Also, several English airmen had come down in the district, and the extra suits could be most useful for getting them into civvies.

A few days later I was sitting in the Café Vaterland with two other prisoners in civilian clothes. In return for a few choice articles from Red Cross parcels we were as usual getting the best of everything. We had a guard with us, and he could easily have been one of the party, especially as we kept our English very low. I became aware that three girls at a near-by table were eyeing us in a very friendly manner. I wondered what they were: they could not be prostitutes, because Hitler was supposed to have banned the profession, but they were not in any kind of uniform so they were probably married with young children. Still perhaps they were worth cultivating. I turned to the guard, who was rather afraid of me as he knew I was so well in with the German Foreign Office.

"Sonny boy, see if the three women will come over to our table and have a drink with us."

"Certainly, Herr Brown, but what else are you after?"

"Let's see first of all what they are like close up, and whether they are friendly towards us."

"Very well then, and if you are fortunate enough to get invited home by them I should like to leave you and meet you just before we return to the camp. I know I can trust you to look after the other two." It seemed that sonny boy was off to see his own girlfriend.

The women accepted the invitation, and I found myself next to one who introduced herself as Gisela Maluche; she had been married, was now divorced, and had a wine shop in Berlin, which sounded promising. Soon the party began to get very gay, with all of us slightly high, much to the envy of people sitting at the other tables. When it was time to leave, Gisela said I was welcome to go back to her flat with her.

"But what about the others?" I said. "We have to keep together tonight."

"I would prefer it if we went back alone, for there is nobody in the flat."

"I'm afraid it's impossible, but perhaps I can see you again?"

"It doesn't matter then; tell your friends to come back as well and we can have a little drink together, on condition you promise to see me again tomorrow."

"I will if I can, but why?"

"Because I have taken a fancy to you, and I think we can have some happy times together."

"I'm sure we can!"

And I meant it, for Frau Maluche fitted in perfectly with the injunction to find a nice girl. God knows I was longing for the physical part of it. I felt, too, that Nan would understand, for it might help me dodge the barbed-wire mentality which had afflicted so many. Anyhow I could write and tell Nan.

Outside the café we purchased bags of chestnuts, and while the guard went off to a little bit of lovemaking with his own girlfriend, the rest of us walked along arm in arm, chewing nuts. As Gisela's flat was in the Meinkoln district of Berlin we went to Potsdamer Platz underground station, and at the other end there was a five-minute walk to Leniestrasse 6 where Gisela lived. Drinks and some *Würst* containing sardines was produced, then one of the girls who lived in the same block departed with her prisoner, leaving just four of us in the room darkened by a power cut. It did not take long for the other two to make full use of the camp bed in the room; but as I put my arm round Gisela she said, "Couldn't you wait until we are alone? It will be so much nicer, and I am sure another day's wait will not hurt you."

I felt ashamed to think that at the first touch of a woman I could barely contain myself, and I was thankful I had been paired off with Gisela. For the next twenty minutes we sat talking, and she was amazed to learn I was a P.O.W. able to get around alone in Berlin. She did not ask any awkward questions but made it clear she was a loyal German utterly convinced that Hitler was going to win the war. She said we would just have to forget our nationalities and become good friends, as it was obvious we were both seeking the same thing.

When the other fellows had finished their wooing we left the flat and met the guard as prearranged. He was in a very bad temper as his girlfriend had been out, and while he had been waiting she had returned with another soldier. He vowed he was finished with women until he got home the coming weekend to his own wife in Bavaria.

Being kept busy I did not see Gisela for some time. Then one evening Tom Cooper and another fellow from the camp staff suggested we should go into town and on the tiles. We soon found ourselves back at the Café Vaterland and met Gisela and her friends. The previous performance was repeated and back we went to the flat. Tom Cooper had a gramophone stolen from the Y.M.C.A., so this time we had music and danced and drank until the early hours of the morning. I sensed that Gisela was getting closer than ever to me, and I wished I could throw caution to the winds, particularly as I felt her warm body inviting me as we danced to the old tunes. When the time came for us to get ready to leave, Gisela could stand the strain no longer and pleaded with me to stop the night, or what remained of it. I said I had to get back to camp, but she appealed to Cooper who said he would arrange it for me if I wanted to stay out all night. I tried to explain to Gisela that it was not that I didn't want to spend the night with her, but that I felt I might compromise her too much if Heimpel found out where I had been staying. But her temper flared when she found my mind was made up, and she picked up the gramophone and heaved it at me. I saw it coming and dodged, and the gramophone went crashing to the floor. Cooper's face was a picture as he picked up the pieces. I felt certain he would never want to visit Leniestrasse 6 again.

The next day I made a point of finding Gisela, and when we got back to the flat we were alone for the first time. As is usual when two people attracted to each other are shut away from the world together, things happened, and so started an association which was to continue for several months and yield much.

Dr Ziegfeld was aware of my friendship with Frau Maluche. One day when we were talking he told me he was having great difficulty in finding a housekeeper; things were extremely awkward for him as his wife and children had been evacuated from Berlin (their house was in the danger zone near Tempelhof Aerodrome), and what added to the awkwardness was the fact that he was responsible for the house next door where there were several Englishmen working on the German side. I saw this was a golden opportunity to get new information, if only I could persuade Gisela to take on the housekeeping work; there was nothing for her to do in the wine-shop trade now that the place had been reduced in an air raid to rubble.

If she took the job it would mean I would be able to see her more often, as I could come to Ziegfeld's house on the pretext of seeing him. He would be discreet enough to leave us alone as much as possible. My hope was that he would leave some of his "England Kommittee" papers lying around.

Gisela agreed, and I found I was indeed able to combine a little tender lovemaking with hard research work, especially into what was going on in the house next door. By now Gisela trusted me implicitly, and unwittingly she often told me things she had overheard.

One day when Ziegfeld was away and Gisela was cleaning it out, I was able to get into the house and found a number of documents incriminating the Englishmen. After reading one document, I decided I *had* to get back to Blechhammer.

Soon after Julius Green had come to E/3 he had told me much about his former naval camp, Mahlag-Milag Nord. I remembered he had mentioned a naval engineer called

Purdy; he had the reputation of being extremely pro-German so that when he eventually vanished from the camp he was suspected of having gone over to the German side. But the Germans stated he was being taken away for punishment for having escaped from a previous camp. I already knew from Ziegfeld that one of the English living next door was a naval officer, though Ziegfeld had not told me his name.

Amongst the documents was one written to the German Foreign Office in which the writer gave his reasons for wanting to work on the German side; these included conviction that Hitler's cause was right, that the combined capitalistic strength of America and Britain had forced the war on the peace-loving Germans; and that Communism would conquer the world if the might of Germany were broken. The letter concluded with "Heil Hitler" and was signed W. Purdy. Provided the letter, which was in longhand, really was Purdy's handwriting, it seemed to provide more than enough proof of what he was up to. Since he came from Green's old camp, and as I had so much work on my hands at the moment, I decided to let Green deal with this matter himself.

To allay suspicion for wanting to return to Blechhammer, I suggested to Heimpel that if they could arrange for me to visit the Y.M.C.A. German Headquarters at Sagan in Silesia, I could get more supplies for Genshagen and also convince the Y.M.C.A. leaders that the Germans were running the holiday camp from a purely idealistic viewpoint. Heimpel, whilst believing I was still ignorant of the British Free Corps, still had doubts about my loyalty towards his Führer, and closely questioned me again. But I finally satisfied him that my blue eyes really were a sign of simplicity. Then I told him that, when in Silesia, I would also like to visit my old camp, Blechhammer E/3, to see some of my friends there. Immediately suspicion clouded his face.

"But Mr Brown, don't you realize it would not be safe for you to go back to Blechhammer? They have threatened to kill you if you ever return!"

"But why should they want to harm me, Major Heimpel?"

"Because they are quite sure you are working for the enemy. Of course that's us your friends mean, isn't it, Mr Brown?" he added with a sneer.

I ignored the implication of his remark. "Are you certain they said they would kill me? That's a very strong word."

"No, they did not actually say the word 'kill'. What one of the English Control Staff said to Paymaster Brauner was that if ever you 'put your ruddy nose through the door of Room 3 again', he and several others would 'do you in'. We understand that to mean they would dispose of you."

"I'm quite sure I've nothing to fear," I said. "They will welcome me back as soon as I tell them all about the good work we are doing at Genshagen and how so many prisoners are benefiting from the Christian side of the camp."

From the expression on Heimpel's face he appeared to be thinking, "What a bloody fool this man is!" So, to convince him further that I was a complete simpleton, I went a step further. "Why not give me permission to invite the Blechhammer staff, the band and concert party to come to Genshagen and let them see for themselves that everything is genuine and above board in the holiday camp. I'm quite sure we must impress upon all camps that all is well in Genshagen. The best way to do that is to have concert parties in from camps all over Germany. Genshagen will gain valuable entertainment, and you will get people in from everywhere."

"What do you mean by that remark?"

"Simply that you would like all and sundry to know of the good work the Germans are doing in our holiday camp."

Heimpel, convinced of my utter greenness, saw I was offering to do the very thing he had been afraid to do—bring people in from everywhere. On my side, I could see my dream of a counter-espionage network linking all the Stalags in Germany coming a little closer to reality.

The morning I left Berlin for Silesia in March 1944, I was in a happy mood, for here I was on my way back to my old camp along with Heimpel's blessing.

My first call was to the Y.M.C.A. Headquarters in Sagan. There I was saddened by the news of the great escape from Sagan R.A.F. camp which had ended so tragically, many of the escapers shot by the Gestapo. Later that day I went to the camp with the Y.M.C.A. representative. The air was tense with horror and hatred. Had they known of my close links with strange German schemes they would have torn me apart.

Later that evening my guard and I left for Blechhammer via Breslau, Oppeln and Hydebreck. In E/3 I faced the usual barrage of questions; and there were now even greater doubts in the minds of my old room-mates. Strangely enough, though, most of the men in the camp seemed pleased to see me again, particularly when they discovered I might arrange for them a holiday trip to Berlin. But first I had wanted to see Julius Green and asked to call on him in BAB 21 on the pretext of having a dental check. While he kept his mouth shut I opened mine. I told Julius exactly where Purdy was living and also what work he was doing for the Germans. He thanked me for the information and promised to send the usual messages home. Before leaving I made tentative arrangements for the visit of the band and *The Mikado* to Berlin. But my own room-mates resisted the plan, for they could not envisage their own camp for six weeks with no music and no plays, and all actors and musicians gone to Berlin in the fifth year of the war.

What I pity I could not tell them there was so much more hinging on this visit to Berlin! I left Blechhammer still determined to have the band and *The Mikado* there—one hundred players in all. It was the only way to get the next stage of my plan moving.

# 10

# My Luck Runs Out

Soon after my return to Genshagen I made a point of seeing Gisela, who was very worried, thinking I might not come back to Berlin. As usual she made me welcome and tried to prove that absence makes the heart grow fonder. But she found that I was angry and depressed—no mood for love-making.

At first she suspected I had found someone else; but after a time I could contain myself no longer and told her all I had seen and heard in Sagan. Then I told her about the Jews in the Blechhammer area, how we had seen the poor devils made to work until they could stand no more, how we had sometimes been forced to witness them being hanged, and how we had seen lorryloads of them, men, women and children, being carted away to Auschwitz. That night I felt I could no longer keep up the pretence of being pro-German. Having had my say I realized she could well repeat all this to somebody in the Foreign Office, and if she did it would be curtains for me. But I did not care, for I felt a strange cleanness in my mouth.

At first Gisela did not speak, then I saw tears in her eyes. She came across to me, and put her arms around me. "John, I have wondered about you for a long time, because I am in love with you, and I am not sure whether you are working as a secret service agent for Britain; but if you are, do all you can to smash Hitler!"

I hastily assured her I was just an ordinary P.O.W.

"You can still help your people win the war," she replied. "I believe what you have told me, and I am ashamed of my own nation."

Gisela was not the only German national to whom I owed much. Back in July 1943, when I was trying to set up the holiday camp, I had met Frau Margarete Langfelder who had a music shop in Berlin and supplied us with a number of instruments. In due course they went on to other camps where it was impossible to buy any. Frau Langfelder I discovered was a bitter anti-Nazi. They had killed her Jewish husband and she longed for the day when Germany would be freed from Hitler. Although she knew nothing of my intelligence activities, she supplied me with much information about the people in Berlin which I was able to send home. She was furthermore instrumental in helping escaped prisoners, not only supplying suits of clothing but also hiding them in her villa. I frequently helped prisoners escape who had fallen foul of the Germans and had been sentenced to long terms in concentration camps. I would hide them in Genshagen until preparations had been made for their escape.

One case concerned a corporal of the Royal Welch Fusiliers who had been sentenced to ten years for intimacy with a Fraülein. He had escaped and returned to his old camp Blechhammer E/3 until the searches, even there, became too hot. Their band brought him to me (a distance of over 500 miles) in their music box along with the hundred others that came to give their production of *The Mikado* in Berlin.

He stayed in hiding at Genshagen for many weeks, until the Gestapo became interested; and then Frau Langfelder hid him for four months until it was safe for him to make a getaway. He eventually reached England.*

Air attacks on Berlin were increasing in frequency and intensity. I would often return to the camp tired after a day in Berlin and not a little frightened. The German A.R.P. service was practically non-existent, and any bodies under ruined buildings stayed there; the stench of the dead added to the horror.

One day I had been into Berlin to contact a number of Swiss and Norwegian journalists, marvelling that men so anti-Nazi were allowed the freedom of the town. Our meeting was suddenly broken up by an air raid, and I found myself in a shelter under the Eden Hotel with a Swiss journalist, Lydia Oswald, who told me she would be visit-

---

* After the war, in 1946, I took up Frau Langfelder's case with the British authorities, for she wished to be allowed to retain her shop in the British sector of Berlin, and also to start up her business again. I later had the pleasure of welcoming her to England.

ing Genshagen at the invitation of the Germans, and was going to write an article on it for a Swiss magazine. She said she was anxious to find out the truth about the camp for it was exciting questions all over the world. She assured me that her report would be a fair one, whatever the consequences. Bombs were falling all around us, but I had to keep my wits about me lest she was trying to trap me into giving information which she would pass on to the Germans. She appeared to be sincere though. The raid went on for what seemed to be hours, and after a time we adjourned to Lydia's room and while we waited for the all-clear drank schnapps, raising our glasses to the gallant R.A.F. and vilifying Hitler and his fellow maniacs.

By the time the raid was over, it was too late to get a train back to Lichterfelde Ost, and in any case most of the central lines were out of action. There was only one thing to do and that was to walk home. On the way I had to pass Goebbels' headquarters, and as I walked past the main entrance I was challenged by a guard. After some difficulty I was able to satisfy him that I was a foreign worker stranded through the raid. He confirmed that Potsdamer Platz station was out of action, which meant that I really was in for a long walk. I handed him a few cigarettes (I had exchanged some Players for some Swiss ones from Lydia Oswald), and he must have been a little puzzled to see they were English and Swiss.

As I walked through the streets of Berlin I saw that the desolation was complete. Buildings had fallen across the streets and blocked the way. Other buildings were in flames; it was nerve-shattering to hear the cries of the people trapped inside them. The heat from the flames was unbearable and I left the doomed party of the city as soon as I could.

Fearing there might be special sabotage checks on in the streets I decided to make my way to the railway and follow the line. It was quite dark when another raid warning came whining from the sirens. The bombs fell almost at once, and I appeared to be right on target. The railway lines suddenly curled up in front, and splinters began to fall around me. I alternately pressed myself flat to the ground and ran as fast as my legs would carry me, for there was no shelter anywhere. I was frightened stiff. A bomb whistled near and down I went. There was a deafening crash, then I rose like a frightened rabbit, just in time to see the remains of a gasometer disappearing in flames a quarter of a mile away.

Both my nerve and wind had gone; I could go no further. Then I realized I was near a station and saw empty carriages in a siding. Oblivious to the fact that they presented an excellent target I climbed into the first carriage, stretched myself out on the seat and fell fast asleep. Next morning when I woke up I quietly left the train and mingled with the crowd on the platform. My dirty appearance aroused no interest for most travellers still showed signs of the battering.

I entrained to Lichterfelde Ost, and as I left the electric train to board the steam train for Grossburen I was confronted by Tom Cooper.

"You're under arrest. You must come along with me to Major Heimpel."

"What's the idea of this?"

"You're suspected of spying."

That was all the information I could get out of him. It was not long before I found myself in the presence of Major Heimpel. First I was stripped naked and my clothing was almost torn apart for evidence against me. I was then allowed to dress and escorted into another room where to my dismay I found myself confronted by two Gestapo men as well as Dr Ziegfeld and Major Heimpel. I was closely cross-examined for over two hours. Where had I been all night? Whom had I been with? Was it true that I was meeting British spies in Berlin? I told them I had been with my girlfriend Gisela Maluche in the early part of the evening, and had then been caught up in the raid. I knew that a check with Gisela would prove my statement and I was anxious to cover up the fact of my meeting with the Swiss and Norwegian journalists. I thought I was doing quite well.

"Brown, I am accusing you of being a secret service agent."

"How can I be, Major Heimpel? I am a prisoner of war, running a special camp for you."

"We have evidence here to prove that you are sending messages home to England."

"You have always disliked me, Major Heimpel and I presume this is your method of getting me out of the way."

"Herr Ziegfeld, I would ask you to read the statement you have there," said Heimpel.

Ziegfeld gave me a long, sorrowing look and picked up the paper which was on the table. He read:

As agreed with you, I went to the camp and found that Green had been sent there as a suspected Jew. It was arranged by the German authorities for me to go in the same barrack room as Green, and before long we were able to meet. Before I had a chance to question him as you wished, he turned on me and said, "I know you are working for the German side so keep away from me."

"Don't be a silly fool, you know as well as I do that I'm a P.O.W. like yourself—weren't we in the same camp together?"

"Yes, but I know you are working for the Jerries in Berlin now, and I can even tell you where you are living as a civilian."

"Well, this is interesting—how did you find all this out?"

"Brown in Berlin told me. You think he is friendly with the Germans, but he is a good fellow really. He is a secret service agent, and has already reported you to England for your Nazi actions!"

And so it went on. I realized that I was indeed trapped unless I could think very quickly. As soon as Ziegfeld had finished I told him I thought Purdy had written the note. He agreed at once but did not show me the paper.

"Well, what have you to say about this?" he continued. "It seems very black against you, and you know that the penalty for spying is death."

"But surely you realize what is happening?" I said, trying to play for a little more time.

"I know what will be happening very shortly," snarled Heimpel.

"I am surprised that you have been taken in by this fellow Green. You know he is a Jew, and you know that the Jews hate the Genshagen camp for they don't want to see any friendship between the prisoners and the Germans. Can't you see they are trying to discredit me so as to break up

Genshagen holiday camp and ruin all the work I am trying to do?"

The two Gestapo men looked at each other significantly, and one of them turned to me and said, "*Donnerwetter*, you're right. This is an attempt by the Jews to discredit you; but we won't let them do it! You are free to leave here. This Jew will be punished for his lies."

I went to leave the room; but Heimpel called me to his private room. He surveyed me with the utmost disdain.

"Well, Brown, you can consider yourself lucky you have scraped through *this* time. Personally, I still think you are a secret agent, and I am going to do my utmost to trap you. Give me one chance to catch you, and I will have you sent to Belsen Camp—that is a slower death than shooting! I know how your people send their messages home, so if you try to send any more you will be caught red-handed. Now get back to the camp, and mind you go straight there."

I was a very worried man, for if what Heimpel had said was true then my work was at an end. I decided to test the truth of his assertion, and sent a number of messages home that weekend. It was not until after the war that I discovered my messages arrived home quite safely, so Heimpel was a damned liar.

Fearful lest Heimpel would try to put him on the spot as a friend of the doubtful Englishman, Dr Ziegfeld for a time showed a marked reserve towards me, going so far as to refuse to talk to me on train journeys or to shake hands with me when we met. He told me it would be unwise for me to use my Foreign Office passport for the time being as Heimpel was obviously hot on my trail, although he (Ziegfeld) was convinced of my integrity. He explained to me that his apparent coldness was only temporary as his work on the England Kommittee was becoming increasingly difficult in view of the hardening of feeling against the English prisoners since the start of the major air raids.

After that searing interview with Heimpel, and feeling thankful I was still free even after sending those messages home despite Heimpel's warning, I thought it wise to appear to acquiesce with Ziegfeld's wish and not use my pass, but give more time to organizing the holiday camp and go out only with a guard.

Most guards were unaware of the traumatic interview I

had been through; and it was not difficult with my cigarettes and chocolate to make them go wherever I wanted. I still changed into civilian clothing whenever I met any German artistes who came to Genshagen Camp to perform or give lectures, for none of them wanted to be seen with a man in the hated British uniform.

All that Ziegfeld's ban meant was that I had to leave the camp with a guard; and so long as I returned with him later in the day all was well. If I wanted to see Gisela I simply sent the guard off and he knew where to find me when it was time to go back. It did not occur to him that I might slip out on my own for part of that time, for he imagined I had a one-track mind like him and would not waste any time away from Gisela. Indeed during this period my work in no way suffered for by now my staff were well trained to keep their eyes open. I still sent messages home.

On 20th July 1944, the Stauffenberg *putsch* against Hitler failed. Himmler and his Gestapo seized supreme power: the Nazis thirsted for revenge against the German Officer Corps of the Wehrmacht. Roland Freisler and his brutal People's Court hauled many leaders for pseudo-trials as a prelude to hanging from piano wires that slowly tightened round their necks.

In all the full horror of the final death-throes of the Nazi regime we P.O.W.s were forgotten. During the autumn, even as the Russians advanced to Warsaw and into East Prussia, Genshagen continued its absurd paradox of holidays for British prisoners who had worked well for Hitler. Ian Ryburn strengthened our morale and determination to survive the war and Jimmy Newcomb strengthened our supplies of canteen goods.

After Arnhem the Allies' advance in North Europe petered out and we were again faced with yet another winter in Germany.

In late December 1944, the Gestapo finally remembered us and swooped on Genshagen. The camp was again searched and this time enough was discovered to convince them that all was not going smoothly in their precious paradise for tired British P.O.W.s. They went through everything.

I was determined they would never search all my personal

papers, many of which would be needed in England after the war. One by one they took us from the room. At last only four of us were left—Jimmy Newcomb, Reg Beattie, Ian Ryburn and me.

The guard took Jimmy and did him over. Ian Ryburn turned to me. "It looks like trouble for you, John," he said. I smiled, and whispered to Beattie. He moved round to the inner wall and started to bait the Jerry, who now had his back to the window. In a second I lifted my important suitcase through the window into Newcomb's arms outside and so to the pile of luggage already searched.

Beattie and Ryburn went next and when my turn came I said innocently, "I've nothing to declare, Heil Hitler!"

That same day they took us to a Berlin Straff prison. There we remained for three weeks, eight to a room. Even though we were closely guarded, we soon smuggled in cards to pass away the time. Christmas and New Year were bleak.

Because of continued bombing, the guards soon became slack. I now had almost as much freedom as before, except that my movements were always by night. I provided myself with a fake pass which stated I was a member of the S.S. and had my photograph on it properly stamped. It was signed by Himmler.

Then in the third week of 1945 Ryburn, Newcomb, Austin, Blewitt, and I were sent back east by train to Lamsdorf, Upper Silesia. One of the first men I met on entering the Stalag was John Borrie, now surgeon at Lazarett-Lamsdorf.

There was unease everywhere. The lightning Russian advance, the P.O.W. camps marching west from Kattowitz and heading into the Sudeten Hills, meant the Third Reich was at long last crumbling. In the appalling confusion my hope was to "disappear" from the Gestapo, and somehow reach England.

# 11

# *Great Trek West*

The Russian fighters, dull compared with the shimmering Superfortresses over Berlin, were now making hourly sweeps over Lamsdorf. No German planes rose from the near-by aerodrome.

Every time our German guards tried to have a roll-call—always a farce in this camp where so many men were in hiding from other camps—the planes swept over and the guards vanished. There was no ack-ack. We waved to the Russian airmen who dipped their wings in greeting.

Soon the guards began to disappear altogether. It would have been easy for us to cross to the Russian lines which were being consolidated ten miles away on the east bank of the Oder River, but it was strange that so few went that way especially as the alternative was a forced march across Germany with the Germans; but the P.O.W.s preferred the devil they knew!

The great trek west began on 22nd January 1945, in bitterly cold weather with snow thick on the ground. Many sensing this would happen had improvised sleighs from the wooden bunks in their barracks and had loaded them with their few possessions—blankets, precious books, photographs sent from their loved ones at home, spare clothing, and what Red Cross food that had been issued that day.

For weeks in Lamsdorf now food had been extremely scarce: we were starved. Even water was rationed, which meant lining up for an hour to get a bucketful for all purposes. Few P.O.W.s were fit for a normal walk, let alone a 600-mile trek across Germany in the worst possible winter conditions, harassed by Allied bombers and and ground-strafing fighters by day and at night huddling together in a snow-clad field.

I can never forget watching the motley crew walking through those gates. For five years they had been shut against most. Now they were flung open so that all could pass out and face perhaps a bomb or death through cold, exhaustion, or a bullet from some fanatical German. Napoleon's retreat in 1812–13 had little on this. I wondered how many would make it home. But as they marched they were a happy throng.

The guards tried to take the sleighs away but after arguments we persuaded them not to interfere. The Germans were so scared of the on-coming Russians that we could threaten them with dire consequences when we finally met our own troops. Insults hurled at the P.O.W.s by the guards as they marched through the gates were returned with interest.

With a heavy heart I joined at the end of the long line of 2,000 men. I vividly recalled that march eastward from France in 1940, and had no intention of repeating it in conditions ten times worse. I knew one or two nights in snow under a frosty moon would bring on fibrositis, perhaps something worse. But above all I did not want to come to a sticky end with victory so near.

A few hours before I had received news that a strict lookout would be kept for P.O.W. 11953 B.Q.M.S. John Brown who—if found—was to be transported *sofort* to Gestapo Headquarters in Berlin where he was wanted on spying charges. The message was marked 'To All Camps' and signed by Himmler. The friend who told me said it was too late for the Germans to have a check-up in Lamsdorf for the Russians had overrun Upper Silesia; but every camp on the marching route would be on the lookout for me. Luckily I slipped through the gates unrecognized, simply because most of the high-ranking Nazi Germans who knew me had already decamped west, taking with them as loot all our personal valuables impounded five years before.

I could have changed my identity—it was just a matter of obtaining someone else's P.O.W. disc—so long as I knew which name was on the disc. But the great danger was that some guard would recognize me somewhere on the journey, or perhaps a fellow prisoner would address me by my proper name in front of a German. There was no one I could go to for advice, for by now it had become "each man for himself", and soon would be "survival of the fittest". I decided my best chance lay in making a break for it at the earliest opportunity. It would be dangerous, especially with the Volkssturm—the German home guard raised as a last defence that winter—now armed and told to shoot any suspect on sight. But to remain with the column would be near suicide.

Our advance on the first day was slow because of deep snow and severe strafing by Russian planes. We now had wounded on our hands—and killed—and minimal medical supplies. It was impossible to break away, for we were in the German front line; S.S. troops would give escaping prisoners short shrift. That night we slept in open fields, so tired we did not care about the cold or worry about freezing to death. They awakened us early next morning; the Germans were anxious to place as great a distance as possible between themselves and the Russians following hard behind. That morning we had another air raid, Allied bombers this time, mistaking us for retreating German troops; but there were fewer casualties.

By midday we reached a British P.O.W. camp in the area where the men were lined up ready to join us on our journey west "to freedom". They shepherded us into the camp and the lucky ones in front received some acorn coffee. The Camp Kommandant—a nasty German bully—then addressed us: he had instructions to take us away from the Russian Front for the German Government wished to continue their protection of us until such time as we could be handed over to the British authorities. We could stay behind if we wished, but in that case the Germans could accept no responsibility. Conditions on the journey might be extremely arduous and no transport was available because our own— British—planes had smashed the German railway and bombed road transport. There would be little food for some time to come. But the Reich would do its utmost to protect us as it had always done to date. Jimmy Newcomb, standing next to me, spat violently, and I gave him a reproachful look.

The Kommandant continued: "I have a message for a prisoner if he is here—B.Q.M.S. John Brown." Involuntarily I began to step forward, but Jimmy's firm grip on my arm brought me to my senses. "We cannot wait now to check all identity discs, but at a later stage of the journey there will be a full check with photographs."

There was no doubt about it, we had to get moving within the next few hours. "We", because Jimmy knew that once I was caught he would be implicated up to the neck. Quite apart from his covering of me he had practically controlled the British black market in Berlin, and also had his past dealing in food tickets at Blechhammer.

Our trepidation would have been even greater had we been aware of an incident in Berlin some two days before this. Margery Booth, who till then had received full protection from the German authorities—having a personal assurance from both Hitler and Goebbels that, were she insulted at any time because of her British birth they would deal with the matter personally—was finally arrested in her flat and taken for interrogation to Gestapo Headquarters. For three days she was grilled and tortured. What was her friendship with the English prisoners at Genshagen? Why did John Brown visit her flat *and* the Berlin State Opera House, apparently unknown to the authorities? What part had she played in helping send messages to England? How was it that the British Free Corps had been a failure? What did she know about the background of John Brown? And how had she helped Jim Newcomb and John Brown to get such connections in the Berlin black market?

Margery denied helping the English prisoners and said she had no connection whatever with me apart from arrangements for concerts at Genshagen. Fortunately by this time she had buried my secret papers where they were never likely to be found—in the grounds of the castle of the Crown Prince, "Little Willie", who happened to be her friend. The questioners then became exasperated and revealed their hand.

"We know that Brown is an English secret service agent, so you need not tell us any more lies. He is under arrest and has revealed the method he employed for getting messages home. His confession has implicated you. We are going to shoot Brown, and then deal with you later—as a German citizen—in the People's Court!"

Margery, with recollections of the manner in which the men involved in the attack on Hitler's life in July 1944 had been executed and films showed publicly—pinned to posts and slowly strangled with piano wire—might easily have broken down under this torrent of lies. But she remained outwardly calm, and demanded to see me to confront me with what she called my lies. This request stumped the Germans. They wished they had said I had already been shot. So they let Margery go, telling her that her every movement would be watched, and that sooner or later they would produce me and provide first-hand proof of her guilt.

Naturally it was only after the end of the war that I heard this, and how Margery had been able to escape during one of the twice-daily air raids on Berlin and had made her way to Bavaria with Gisela Maluche, where they had remained until picked up by the Americans. Margery later handed my secret papers intact to the British authorities to whom they proved of great use,* although in the main Old Bailey trials my tiny copy papers were allowed as court exhibits, on the assumption that the originals had been lost.

On the second day of the march, during a vicious raid that had scattered us far and wide, Jimmy and I made our dash for freedom. Most of the guards had their heads buried in the snow as bombs dropped all around. We made for a nearby pine forest, knowing that S.S. could be there but feeling a German bullet would hurt no more than an Allied bomb— provided it killed us outright. We passed through the wood without encountering S.S., and came upon a tiny deserted village, strangely silent, with no sign of life. But in a lane off the narrow street stood a large German staff car.

We stood on the corner talking and watching for people to appear; but nothing happened. We decided to pinch the car. We agreed that I would walk down the street past the car; if the key was in the ignition we would jump in and drive off.

I walked down the road while Jimmy remained on look-out round the corner. I glanced into the car as I passed but could see no key. I sauntered to the end of the road and back again. I opened the door. Incredibly the key *was* there. I was just climbing in when the door of the house opposite opened and an S.S. colonel rushed out, fumbling for his revolver. He had almost reached me—near enough to see murder in his eyes—when Jimmy sprung on his back, knocking the gun from his hand. In a flash I went to

---

* By way of a reward for what she did for England, Margery was given back her English nationality after I had personally taken up her case with the British authority.

Jimmy's aid; and, although the German fought bravely, two against one finished him.

We knew that the road we had walked along ran parallel to the route along which the prisoners were marching, so we decided to drive straight on. It was a strange sight: a German staff car racing over the countryside, driven by an unkempt British P.O.W., while his co-driver—dressed in khaki—had an S.S. colonel's hat perched on his head.

Half an hour later, still driving on inches of snow, we stopped to check petrol and found thirty gallons in cans, a suitcase containing a Wehrmacht and an S.S. colonel's uniform, and shaving kit. Under the back seat there was enough German canned rations to last a week, and in the dashboard pocket maps covering much of Germany. It was our lucky day, and our finds gave us courage. Like many others, our S.S. colonel had clearly decided to abscond west from the front line, and had provided himself with an ordinary Wehrmacht uniform lest he run into Allied troops. Not that it would have helped for, as an S.S. man, he could never lose the tell-tale branded marks on his arm.

Studying the map we found we were near our old camp Blechhammer E/3, whence it would be possible to follow a good road heading south-west through Slovakia and Austria in the direction of Switzerland or, better still, towards the American troops out west near Nuremberg.

Blechhammer was as desolate as any village we had seen on the way. The Germans were doing what the French had done in 1940—evacuating homes and loading their possessions on to handcarts. These Germans, disciplined to the end, jumped to attention and gave us the Nazi salute as our staff car drove by. By this time Jimmy had dressed as a Wehrmacht private while I looked a passable S.S. colonel, even though the jacket was tight in the arms and the trousers chafed my crutch.

Arbeits Kommando E/3 shocked us: American pattern bombers had done their worst: there was barely a hut standing. Across the Adolf Hitler Canal we could hear the rumble of heavy artillery—the Russians were coming nearer. As we drove towards the Baustelle we remembered those bitterly cold mornings when we had to trudge along this very road for our *Arbeit für Deutschland*. By car it took us a mere five minutes. But what we saw was a sight for sore eyes. For five years 20,000 P.O.W.s and workers from all over Europe had been bullied and kicked into helping the German war effort by building this huge petrol-from-coal plant. A few well-directed air raids had destroyed practically everything.

A feeling of self-satisfaction came over me. The bombing had been on target. The maps showing ack-ack and balloon defences I had been sending home had been used to good effect.

My satisfaction was short-lived. We found ourselves facing a road barrier—a checkpoint to ensure that all good Nazis fought to the bitter end. Luckily for us our colonel had provided himself with papers for just such a contingency and we were allowed to proceed on our way after much clicking of heels and Heil Hitlers. We then made for the open road, and apart from one or two similar encounters we had little trouble on our journey.

Finally after travelling some 300 miles we ran out of petrol somewhere in Bavaria. There was nothing for it but to abandon the car and, as we did not want to be picked up in German uniform with forged papers we got back into our khakis and loaded ourselves with as much food as we could carry. That night, having eaten our fill, we slept in a sheltered glade.

Next morning we started walking, hoping to fall in with one of the many columns now marching on one of two directions—some westward from the Russians, the others eastward from the Americans and English. We passed many civilians; but none challenged us. By now the German population was praying for the end.

Around midday we heard the drone of planes and saw flight after flight raid a nearby target. The planes twisted and turned and glistened in the sunlight—American planes. Guided by a thick pall of smoke we walked towards the town, hoping to find where we were. In an hour we were on the outskirts. A signpost told us it was Regensburg—the great ball-bearing manufacturing centre. We skirted the town and found an old shed for the night. Next morning we saw a familiar sight: barbed wire and guard boxes. The guard boxes were unmanned. The prisoners walked freely in and out of the camp. Jimmy looked at me. Our mouths were watering for a hot drink; snow is fine as a freshener but it warms nothing, and by now our food supply had dwindled.

"Let's get in there and have a decent drink and a kip on a good bed," I said to Jimmy.

"You don't think it might be too dangerous for us?"

"Not if we can rest quietly. And we can always crawl out again if anyone's suspicious of us."

It was Hohenfels, the camp for English N.C.O.s who would not go to work for Germany. It was a remarkable camp, with its bookies' stands and the stalls which reminded me vividly of Petticoat Lane, London, where my office was. Food was scarce, for now no Red Cross supplies could get through from Switzerland. But we soon found friends and were given a heavenly cup of tea. We learned that the Yanks were not far away out west. The bombing we'd seen occurred daily. The railway tracks and yards were now popular bombing targets.

Two days later when walking round the camp we bumped into two sergeants, one English, the other Australian. They had both been in Genshagen and had fallen foul of the Germans on disciplinary grounds.

"So we've caught up with you at last, you bloody Jerry swine," one of them said.

"What d'you mean by that?"

"You wait till you get back to England. You'll have your stripes pulled off you, and we shall be only too pleased to give evidence against you at your court-martial. We know what you've been doing for the Jerries, recruiting men for the Free Corps."

I could be forgiven for having murder in my thoughts; but it was obvious that we could not start trouble here. Jimmy and I moved to another section of the camp. There we became friendly with R.S.M. W. J. Green, who came from Newcastle. He was very good to us and fed us.

With the Americans advancing, the guards were becoming slack and it was easy for P.O.W.s to nip outside and forage for fat chicken, rabbit and fresh eggs. One shepherd grazing sheep near his camp saw several of his flock become roast mutton. We were so hungry we killed and ate the beasts the same day.

One day in early April we were in the village when suddenly fifty S.S. men appeared from nowhere, rounded us all up and trained their machine gun on us. A German general appeared and told the S.S. men to lower their guns. Then he spoke to us through an interpreter. He said that the Allied troops would be in the area within a few days, and that it was his duty as general in charge of the area to hand us over safely to the authorities; but he could not do that if we were wandering around like this. Then he dismissed the S.S. men, and when they had gone spoke to us in perfect English.

"It is possible that the S.S. will fight a rearguard action through this village and they will have *no mercy* on you if they find you here. I want to help you, and I know you will put a good word in for me when your troops arrive." He then held up a slip of paper on which was written that he had been good to English P.O.W.s

Some of our guards had asked for similar slips; but they had usually been given a note saying, "The bearer of this note has been a P.O.W. guard. He has been a perfect swine—treat him the same!" But we went back to our camp that night happy to think that at least one German general knew the meaning of the word decency.

Day by day we waited for the Americans. One morning the German guards, Kommandant and all, marched up to us, stood rigidly to attention and asked us to take them over, and give them any job we liked until we were freed. The latrines needed attention; there were potatoes to peel; the camp needed cleaning. It was good to see Germans now doing these tasks. But strangely enough I did not see one of our men ill-treat the Germans or poke fun at them. Perhaps we felt sorry for them; their durance vile had yet to start; and it lasted long.

Next day I was walking alone outside the camp, and came upon the famous Hohenfels Military Barracks, now deserted. I went inside to look around: the place was a shambles. Pictures of Hitler—the glass broken—and the other top Nazis, hung on the wall, thick crayon marks disfiguring the faces. Tables and chairs were smashed, and papers strewn over the floor. Then I heard a voice behind me, "So this is how your wonderful race treats a conquered nation?" There was a sinister note in the voice, and I swung round quickly. A fat German officer, with as square a head as any I had seen, was pointing a revolver at me; his intention was plain. For a moment I was tongue-tied and simply could not think what to do. For once I had been doing no harm, yet I was in greater danger than ever before. Then a miracle happened. Another English prisoner walked through the door with a heavy iron chandelier in his hand. He sized up the situation and brought the object down on the German's head. There was a horrible crunching noise, and a slumping. When I looked around again my saviour had gone: and I did not see him again. I thanked him for saving my life.

On 17th April Hohenfels was evacuated, the Germans allowing the sick men to stay behind until the Allies arrived. There were three good reasons why Jimmy and I decided we were sick. First, we had had enough of walking to last us for a very long time; second, we had no desire to walk to the area where Hitler had announced his intention of forming a redoubt and fighting to the very last; and third, we knew Hitler had issued an order that all Allied P.O.W.s were to be liquidated as they were a danger to the German public and were also causing far too much sabotage. The local Kommandant had refused to obey this order; but the nearer they got to the place where the last stand would be made, the more chance there was of the order being carried out.

The problem was that the Germans had no food to leave for us and our only hope was to forage in the village and in the German store houses. This we did, and found ourselves literally living off the fat of the land. It was strange, a few unarmed prisoners, after five long years now being masters of everything.

We waited impatiently for the Yanks to come and worried lest the camp should be taken for a military target and bombed. Jimmy and I, therefore, decided to go out one night reconnoitring. After walking for about three hours, during which we passed through German lines without being challenged, we came upon an advanced American camp, and were able to walk in without the slightest opposition. They gave us a first-class meal and told us they would be taking over Hohenfels in the next three days; we could stay with them if we liked. But after having a good wash and brush-up and filling our pockets with American field rations we made our way back to camp to tell the good news of our early release. By now, all the German troops had melted away.

It was the afternoon of 22nd April 1945 that the Yanks reached Hohenfels. Two jeeps, commanded by a young lieutenant, pulled up at the camp gates, and with little ceremony hoisted a star-spangled banner. But we had forestalled them for we had already unfurled a Union Jack that had been hidden there for almost five years.

And so the crazy war was drawing to its end; the German bubble had been burst; nothing but fear and trembling remained of the master race. For the next three days we wandered round the village as we would; and, as it was a serious offence for the Yanks to do any pillaging, we did it for them. The G.I.s had to admit that fresh eggs and chicken tasted good after their own canned rations.

There were several French forced labour men in the area. They went to the Americans with tales of ill-treatment. I was present when some French produced a very frightened German who admitted he had shot and killed a Frenchman a few months earlier. The French wanted the Americans to shoot the man, but the G.I. said it was against their orders; if, however, they would like to borrow his rifle that would be O.K. This was done. The French made the German dig his own grave before they shot him, which was what the Germans had inflicted on the French in 1940.

We had to apply a good deal of restraint when dealing with these Frenchmen for they had suffered so terribly at the hands of the Nazis. Their homes had been destroyed, their wives and women forced to become bedmates of the master-race. Those who refused had gone to the labour camps of the Third Reich.

The Americans asked the Frenchmen to produce the worst Gestapo men in the district. Then we saw these men taken for a ride which they would never forget. They were made to sit on the bonnet of a jeep, facing the driver, and then the jeeps were driven flat out by the drivers—several of them negroes. The countryside was extremely hilly and as the jeeps came downhill the unfortunate passengers must have been hanging on by their toenails. It was hard to say whether they suffered more from fright or from hot pants.

On 29th April we were taken to a big camp near Nuremberg where they sorted us out, ready for the flight home.

The desolation and ruin in the streets was pathetic; the great historic churches were rubble: no Meistersinger sang.

On 1st May, elated, we reached Erfurt Airport, delighted to find friendly American WAAFS serving proper coffee in proper coffee stalls. One of these was Marlene Dietrich, in full U.S. uniform, but with legs as beautiful as ever. That night we were invited to a party with Miss Dietrich where she and several other film stars with the forces entertained us. It was a wonderful evening, forerunner of all the happy things to come.

It was an enormous relief at long last to be out of the reach of the Nazis: the feeling was indescribable. I began to sort all the notes I knew must be of great value to the British authorities. I hoped my miniature documents were still safe and sound, hidden in my shoe, for they had done much walking since Genshagen.

From Erfurt they flew us to Brussels then handed us over to the British. We filled in a form: name—rank—army number—P.O.W. number—when captured—home address—unit—and could we name anyone who had ill-treated any prisoners—anyone who had worked for the Nazis or any British Free Corps members: all necessary security.

I filled in all parts relevant to myself but marked the latter questions: "Have additional information available when I reach England."

We then lined up to hand papers in, and a quick check was made in the files. When the form was passed the naval officer receiving the papers glanced at a list in front of him. He shook hands with each one in front of me, and congratulated them. Then it was my turn.

They took my form and checked the file. Then the officer looked at his list. His smile changed to a frown; his eyes widened. I had my hand half-ready for the handshake, but he ignored it and told me brusquely to stand to one side. He whispered to an aide standing near.

In a minute a sergeant-major came up and marched me to the Company Office. I was escorted into a room and told that a charge was immediately being laid against me for having aided the enemy. Had I anything to say?

I said some mistake had been made, but that unfortunately I could say nothing until in England. The officer said he knew nothing about the charge, but my flight would be delayed until further orders had been received from SHAEF (Supreme Headquarters Allied Expeditionary Force). In the meantime I would be given a companion-escort who would have to stay with me all the time. Deflated at this poor regard for all I had been through, I tried to keep a level head. Doubtless several men who knew me or my name in Blechhammer or Genshagen had already passed through Brussels and had described me as pro-German. Perhaps the naval officer's list was of people wanted urgently—including those needed by M.I.6—to complete cases against traitors. That night my escort and I toured the cafés, and when we were both tired, we slept in a room specially reserved for such a prisoner as me.

Next morning it was galling to see all my friends leave for the airport while they kept me back while some fool sorted out his mistake. A major said he might possibly be able to help me if I would tell him about what my secret information was. But my instructions had been clear: only in England, and then only to somebody in authority could I talk about my work. He shrugged his shoulders and left. In the afternoon he returned, saying that a high-ranking officer from SHAEF had called. He took me to him. The officer immediately came forward and shook me warmly by the hand.

"Well done, Brown, you've carried out a first-class piece of work. You are required in England and must be flown there as soon as possible."

I thanked him, then asked very quietly whether I was still under arrest. He turned a little pink, while my major friend looked distinctly uncomfortable.

Within twelve hours I was in a plane. It seemed to matter little that we had to lie flat out in the bomb bays. At least we were flying home.

That first sight of England after five and a half long years affected us all. Some wept—their troubles were over, I thought. For myself I knew I still had a great deal of work to do, but the thought of getting home to my wife and child, of having a drink in my local without having to watch for those seeking, suspicious eyes, was too much. I, too, found myself wiping my eyes and blowing my nose to cover my confusion.

We landed at a secret airfield near Horsham, and from there were driven to a special reception camp where WAAFS and WVS girls received us. They tried to make everybody happy and gave us the latest war news. We were then de-loused, given new uniforms, vests and pants, then taken to a huge tent where a superb meal was laid on. After official speeches, lorries were provided and they took us to another large reception camp where we handed in our papers. They told us we could use the telephones to ring home and gave us sufficient money for a good Scotch in the mess. The papers were taken to the Company Office while we remained and listened to BBC news, the first I'd heard in the open for five years. Then the dramatic announcement came—the following day, 8th May 1945, would be V.E. Day (victory in Europe).

They gave details of trucks leaving the camp at 5 a.m. next morning and each hut was told which truck to board.

Then came a message for me to report to the Company Office at once. On my way there I was amazed to meet two members of the British Free Corps, now neatly dressed in British uniforms. They had clearly slipped through the security net, at least for the time being. I met the colonel in charge who greeted me warmly. He had War Office orders that I was to wait until a staff-car came to take me straight up to London.

I thanked him, and told him about the Free Corps men. He was concerned, but said he could do nothing about it, which seemed strange after my own treatment in Brussels. I then phoned home. My wife was in London to meet re-turned prisoners. She had heard that Jimmy Newcomb and Ian Ryburn were home, but could get no news of me. I was told she was very concerned. I left the call-box number and asked that she phone me there at midnight.

I shall never forget the sound of Nan's voice again: we tried to sound natural but it was impossible. She asked me when I would be home. I said I did not know, for the War Office wanted me in London. I thought her heart would break: my own was almost there.

My mind was in a turmoil. It didn't seem fair that I could not go home like the rest. And I still riled at my treatment in Brussels, especially now the Free Corps men were wander-ing around unfettered in England. I could be kept in

London for days. No car had turned up and anyhow what car could get through on V.E. day?

In the mess we drank through the night and on till around 5.30 a.m. just before the trucks left. My plan was now clear. The trucks arrived and the men scrambled happily aboard. There was no truck-check, and when the officer in charge said they were pulling out in five minutes and that anybody not on board then would have to wait hours for later transport, I looked at my watch, gave them four minutes, then jumped on. That minute's wait seemed an age, but the trucks left and in a few minutes we were at Horsham station. By 8 a.m. I was on the Sunbury train from Waterloo.

I opened a newspaper and saw horror pictures of Belsen camp—great piles of dead bodies male and female, they had been starved and then half cremated. A cold shudder ran down my spine. I recalled Heimpel's threat, "We will send you to Belsen!" I had been luckier than I realized.

At Sunbury I gave my ticket to old Dan, permanent porter at the station. He said, "Good morning", then realized who I was. He ran after me and insisted on chatting interminably.

I walked up the road nervously. I had never been so nervous in all those years of dodging the Germans. There was a gap where our local had been bombed. There was nobody about on the road—it was barely nine o'clock and the day was proclaimed a public holiday. I rounded the bend of the road and stopped dead. Ahead were the familiar barbed wire and sentry-boxes, plus hundreds of men in Wehrmacht uniform. Then I realized this was Kempton Park Racecourse which had been converted into a P.O.W. camp for the duration of the war—a camp within thirty yards of my home. This time the Germans were inside the wire—not outside.

I entered my home. I had rehearsed this scene over and over for the last two months; but it never turned out that way. Without any speeches we were in each other's arms. Minutes later Nan said, "Don't you think you ought to take your pack and greatcoat off?"

# 12

# Mission Accomplished

After a week of perfect domestic bliss I had a phone call from the War Office, saying they had been searching for me. Would I report to London! They took my shoes and the papers therein, and gave me clothing-ration coupons for a new pair. They invited me to make a full statement of my activities in Germany—three full days of continuous writing. It ended, "I'm aware that many fellow P.O.W.s thought I was working for the Germans: my whole approach must have made them think so, but what I did was in the best interests of my country." What had happened to me in Brussels still rankled.

After the Treason Trials at the Old Bailey where I gave Crown evidence, one of the heads of M.I.6 said, "Do you know, if all those other prisoners hadn't suspected you of being pro-German, you wouldn't have been doing your job properly! You ought to go down on your knees right now and thank Almighty God that you have come safely through it all." Little did he know I had been doing that for quite some time!

When my statement had been carefully checked I was told that if I wished I could return to my pre-war civilian office work, but would not be discharged from military service until all the cases were cleared up. Nor would I be returned to any military unit while still needed by the War Office.

With many of the staff still on active service, I seemed welcome back at work; but as time passed I found the atmosphere peculiar, not hostile but certainly one of suspicion. When I approached a good friend who was a senior staff member, after some hesitation he said, "Another P.O.W. member of staff has returned before you, John, and told the directors that you spent the war working for the Germans." He had been in an Oflag and had probably heard a few rumours which he had embellished. But it was impossible to tackle him about his statement for the poor fellow died shortly afterwards from privations endured as a P.O.W. But he did much harm, especially as I had been expressly forbidden by M.I.6 officials from mentioning what I'd been doing. They told me to suffer in silence until the Treason Trials were over, then they would clear my name.

In the succeeding weeks, there were visits from M.I.6 officials and further statements all helping to forge links in the chains of prosecution. We had meetings at the War Office and in my home, and I had the pleasure of meeting Commander Burt and Inspectors Davis and Edwards, two Scotland Yard men loaned to the War Office. Then the trials started.

The first was a court-martial at Margate at which I had to give evidence against a New Zealander who to my mind had been one of the ringleaders of the British Free Corps. After he had been captured by our troops he had made a statement in which he said that he had joined the Corps simply to get information for England, and had proceeded to betray his fellow members of the Corps; he had then written at length about my own activities, accusing me of being a highly paid German official. There were enough weaknesses in his statement to prove his guilt, and I was called to corroborate the fact that he had been seen in Berlin in Free Corps uniform. My evidence was given in secret, and as soon as I left the court I was mobbed by reporters, but was unable to comment.

Later, at Walter Purdy's trial at the Old Bailey, my full name, army particulars, and home address were read out in court and I had to reply to a question indicating that I had been a secret service agent in Germany. This time the cat was out of the bag. When the court adjourned photographers and reporters took their toll. Some of the London papers carried photographs showing me being congratulated by high-ranking M.I.6 officials.

In the office next day the directors sent for me and said how proud they were and that, of course, they had never lost faith in me.

Purdy was found guilty of broadcasting for the Germans, and preparing propaganda pamphlets for them. His defence was that he had broadcast in order to escape and pass coded messages to the Air Ministry about weather conditions for raids on Berlin. His death sentence was later commuted.

Tom Cooper's jaw dropped when I entered the witness box for the prosecution at his trial. I did my best for him by saying how he had helped to get information for me, though I was sure he had not approached me before the D-Day landings, of 6th June 1944 when Germany's fate was sealed. On this point, the defence Counsel questioned me closely, saying that with all I had to worry about at Genshagen, was it not possible I was mistaken about the date—as if any P.O.W. could forget the date of D-Day.

Then Sir Hartley Shawcross, the Attorney-General, seized on my statement and said that not only had Cooper seduced his fellow men into joining the Free Corps, but had betrayed the very men he had led into trouble when he realized he was on the wrong side. The death sentence was passed, but commuted to one of life imprisonment. I felt sorry for Cooper, for we had been through many dangerous moments together in Berlin and he had spent many hours in my room at Genshagen and travelling together to and from Blechhammer. He had been so very young at the outbreak of the war.

Then at long last came warm letters from ex-P.O.W.s all over the world apologizing for having doubted me during the war. Somehow they allayed the strain and tension of those weeks of Treason Trials. Relief came with my belated discharge from the Army and return to normal civilian life.

Any lingering doubts were dispelled when I was awarded the Distinguished Conduct Medal for services to the Allied cause. The citation gave some idea of my activities; but it failed to mention all the good luck that came my way. Nor did it mention that I was only able to do what I did because of my Christian belief which sustained me in my durance vile through not only the dangers, but the hopeless dreariness of prisoner-of-war life.

# APPENDIX

## *A Year Passes*★

It is a year since most of us at this working camp left Stalag, and it seems a favourable time for a comparison between then and now.

Most of us were only too eager to get out on work of some sort—can we forget the rushes when the names for working parties were asked for?—for it was felt that the boredom would be much relieved with less time on our hands. Those few days in Stalag seemed like an age without ending, and the thought of months and perhaps years without anything to do was unbearable.

And so we arrived at this large camp. We were for the most part an untidy crowd. For we had not yet recovered from the trials of a long march, and as yet cleaning materials and toilet requisites were not available in any large quantity. Most of us were wearing uniforms which still showed marks of the recent battle, and more than a few were dispirited, wondering what was happening at home, how soon letters would come through, what sort of treatment we would get and, last but by no means least, whether we would ever get used to our new diet. Discipline was sadly lacking, and it looked as if a very bad impression was going to be given of the new British soldier.

However, much has been accomplished in a year, and if all the British P.O.W. camps in Germany have altered as this one has, then we can be proud in the knowledge that once again the ability of the British soldier to adapt himself to any condition, adverse or otherwise, has come to the fore. In this camp we have been extremely fortunate that every assistance has been given us by those in authority over us during

---

★ An article written by Brown for *The Camp* P.O.W. newspaper and published on 7th September 1941.

our captivity, and there is hardly a man who has not appreciated this and responded accordingly. The language difficulty has been overcome to a great extent, and perhaps both sides are beginning to think a little of the other fellow's point of view, which will be all to the good when at last there is peace, and friendship has been restored between the two nations.

Now let us look at the conditions and activities here, which make us justly "camp proud". When considering what is carried out here, it must be remembered that this is a working camp and, except for the evenings and the weekends, the men are away from the camp, and therefore they do not have a surplus of time on their hands.

Thanks to the Camp C.S.M. setting an excellent example, discipline has returned to the men in a remarkable degree, and that has made things much easier. The bugler can be heard at set times of the day, and all the familiar calls such as "Reveille", "Sick Parade" and "Lights Out" are sounded. It is very unusual to see a dirty man in the camp, and as a consequence the general health has improved, and, incidentally, through this, personal living conditions have improved to a large extent. The very low sickness figure in the camp at the moment is a great tribute to the medical staff headed by one of our own Medical Officers.

The camp site itself is kept very clean. We are split up into blocks with six rooms in each and there is great competition between the rooms for originality, neatness, and general appearance both inside the rooms and the surrounding area outside.

The blocks have been given familiar street names such as Mayfair, Red Cross Street (medical rooms), Princess Street, King Street, and Old Kent Road. The latter was originally called Rotten Row, but the name has been changed, as the occupants of the block complained that it was liable to cause some slight misunderstanding. Detail is posted daily under the clock in Trafalgar Square. We can even boast of a "Sauerkraut Villa" and an "Arbeiter's Paradise".

The canteen here is very good, and once again, the authorities assist us in every way to obtain supplies of authorized articles. We have our own Canteen Fund, and money credited to this account is afterwards used for the benefit of everybody in the camp. Articles for room improvement and materials for cleaning are obtained through the canteen and then issued free to the rooms. Men are assisted most liberally when the Medical Officer decided that it is necessary for health reasons for a man to have glasses or special teeth attention. When anybody is without funds through sickness, cigarettes etc. are provided out of the Fund. A contribution is also sent to Stalag each month for the benefit of the wounded there. The balance in hand at the moment is about 600 RM, and more than that amount has already been expended, which undoubtedly proves the success of the scheme.

Concerts are held every Sunday night and also on holidays, and the quality of the entertainment is undeniably very good. The Camp C.S.M. has worked extremely hard to bring about something approaching perfection and he receives valuable assistance from the Medical Officer. There is an excellent band consisting of ten mouth organists, accordionists and baritonists. All are dressed alike. Sketches written by members of the camp have been of a high quality, and there is no lack of comedians. We have our own George Formby, and the straight singers would not disgrace themselves under competitive conditions. There are the usual competitions, such as "Tune Guessing", "Tongue Twisters", "Spelling Bees", and "General Knowledge Questions". The Welsh Choir, recently formed, is going to prove a real item of enjoyment, even though the English members of the audience might be listening to a foreign broadcast when the native tongue is used. A pantomime, written and acted by members of the camp staff, is in the course of production, and judging by the efforts in small sketches by the same groups, we are going to be given something quite out of the ordinary. One of our accordionists has composed a very stirring march entitled "Out of Action", and as a proof of its popularity the tune can be heard whistled on many occasions in the camp. A foxtrot, words and music, called "Thoughts", has also been written and has a great fascination.

At the moment we are trying to obtain new instruments to form one or more new bands, and once again the Canteen Fund will provide the purchase money, should we be lucky enough to get the instruments.

The football pitch, which has been enlarged and is being

levelled off by voluntary workers in the evenings, is in great demand over the weekend. An International Championship is being fought out, and the matches are played on Sunday afternoons before large crowds. As I write, it looks as if Wales will be the first country to hold the shield. The Welsh team have put up a very creditable performance with a limited number to choose from, and have already beaten England and drawn with Scotland. Ireland, too, must be congratulated on raising a team for the competition with barely more than eleven men to choose from. Inter-Regimental and Room Matches are very popular, and the enthusiasm shown by the spectators would not disgrace a London football crowd. Sweepstakes are held on the bigger games, and all the profit handed over to the Canteen Fund.

The rooms find time for Darts, and Chess Matches, and a neat shield has been made which is hung in the window of the champions. A tour of the rooms would show numerous other games in progress.

Within a few months an excellent library has been formed and we have over 600 books in circulation. This number is gradually increased as new copies of famous "Tauchnitz" editions are purchased, while occasionally books are received from the Red Cross and other sources, for which we are most grateful.

The religious side of life is not forgotten. Arrangements have been made for the Catholics to visit the local church in the village once each month, while those of the English faith hold a weekly service on Sunday afternoons.

There is much more that could be mentioned, but sufficient has been said to show that we are "camp proud" here. When we were first made prisoners-of-war, progress in our life seemed to stop; but we have tried to make progress—for our own benefit in our new life. Without a doubt, a lot of knowledge gained and experiences endured will be of value to us when we return to normalcy. To those dear to us at home, we are trying to make the best of things.

We must not forget that although we have our trials they are facing theirs just the same, we hope no worse—at home. Here we have decided that things are only as black as one makes them, and that fact alone accounts for the happy spirit prevailing throughout the camp.

# References

Some of the author's exploits have been described in the following newspapers and books

1 Brown, J. H. O. 'Self-made Spy'. The *Sunday Express*, London, 1st September, 1946, page 5.
2 Brown, J. H. O. 'Dunedin Chaplain—Unique Ordination—Ceremony in Nazi Camp'. *Otago Daily Times*, Dunedin, New Zealand, 23rd August, 1946, page 5.
3 Ryburn, I. G. 'Prison Camp Life: Dunedin Chaplain's Part: Combating German Plans'. *Ibid*, 24th August, 1946.
4 Brown, J. H. O. 'The Man who Fooled the Nazis'. The *Sunday Sun*, Newcastle-upon-Tyne, 1st January, 1946, page 2. *Ibid*, 8th January 1946.
5 West, Rebecca. *The Meaning of Treason*. Macmillan & Co. Ltd, London, 1949.
6 Green, J. M. *From Colditz in Code*, Robert Hale Ltd, London, 1971.
7 Borrie, J. *Despite Captivity—A Doctor's Life as Prisoner of War*. Kimber & Co., London, 1975.

# Glossary of German Words used in the Text

| | |
|---|---|
| *Abort* | Latrine |
| *Abwehr* | Military Intelligence Corps |
| *Arbeit* | Work |
| *Arbeitskommando* | Work-party or work-camp |
| *Ausländer* | Foreigner |
| *Ausweis* | Travel pass |
| *Baustelle* | Building site |
| *Blitz* | Lightning onslaught |
| *Bude* | Brothel or small hut |
| *Deutschland* | Germany |
| *Ersatz* | Substitute |
| *Feldwebel* | R.S.M. or C.S.M. (military rank) |
| *Fräulein* | German maiden |
| *Führer* | Leader |
| *Gauleiter* | Regional leader |
| *Gefreiter* | Corporal |
| *Gestapo* | Secret police |
| *Gute Nacht* | Goodnight |
| *Heil Hitler* | Greeting demanded by the Nazis |
| *Kaputt* | Broken or wrecked |

| | |
|---|---|
| *Kommandant* | Commandant |
| *Kraft durch Freude* | Strength through Joy (a Nazi slogan) |
| *Lager* | Camp or enclosure |
| *Luftwaffe* | German Air Force |
| *Oberschlesischehydrierwerke* | Upper Silesian Hydration Works |
| *Pfennig* | Penny |
| *Raus* | Get out! |
| *Reich* | State |
| *Reichmark* | Hitler's unit of money |
| *Sauerkraut* | Pickled cabbage |
| *Schlafen Sie wohl* | Sleep well! |
| *Sofort* | At once |
| *Sonderführer* | Special leader in Military Intelligence |
| *Stalag* | Military Base Camp |
| *Straffen* | To strafe or punish |
| *Strengstens* | Most strongly |
| *Stube drei* | Room 3 |
| *Über* | Over |
| *Vaterland* | Fatherland |
| *Verboten* | Forbidden |
| *Wehrmacht* | Army |
| *Werkschutz* | Work Police |
| *Würst* | Sausage |
| *Zahlmeister* | Pay-master |

# Index